KT-162-078

Matthew

Tells the Good News

A quick look at this book

This edition of the Gospel of Matthew is taken from the *Holy Bible*, New Living Translation, British text, copyright © 2000, an anglicised version of the *Holy Bible*, New Living Translation.

Holy Bible, New Living Translation, copyright © 1996, by Tyndale Charitable Trust. All rights reserved.

Cover Design by ICP copyright © 2004

The text of the *Holy Bible*, New Living Translation, may be quoted in any form (written, visual, electronic, or audio) up to and inclusive of two hundred and fifty (250) verses without express written permission of the publisher, provided that the verses quoted do not account for more than 20% of the work in which they are quoted, and provided that a complete book of the Bible is not quoted. When the *Holy Bible*, New Living Translation, is quoted, the following credit lines must appear on the copyright page or title page of the work:

Scripture quotations marked (NLT) are taken from the *Holy Bible*, New Living Translation, copyright © 1996. Used by permission of Tyndale House Publishers, Inc, Wheaton, Illinois 60189. All rights reserved.

When quotations from the NLT are used in nonsaleable media, such as church bulletins, orders of service, newsletters, transparencies, or similar media, a complete copyright notice is not required, but the initials (NLT) must appear at the end of each quotation.

Quotations in excess of two hundred and fifty (250) verses or 20% of the work, or other permission requests, must be directed to and approved in writing by Tyndale House Publishers, Inc. P.O. Box 80, Wheaton, Illinois 60189, USA.

New Living, NLT, and the New Living Translation logo are trademarks of Tyndale House Publishers, Inc.

ISBN 0 – 9015.1846 – 8   2004/20M

Published by: The Scottish Bible Society, 7 Hampton Terrace, Edinburgh, EH12 5XU

Typesetting copyright © The Scottish Bible Society.

Typeset in Souvenir BQ by Solidus www.solid-us.com

Printed in Italy by Lego s.p.a.

CHAPTER 1

The Record of Jesus' Ancestors

This is a record of the ancestors of Jesus the Messiah, a descendant of King David and of Abraham:

² Abraham was the father of Isaac.

Isaac was the father of Jacob.

Jacob was the father of Judah and his brothers.

³ Judah was the father of Perez and Zerah (their mother was Tamar).

Perez was the father of Hezron.

Hezron was the father of Ram.*

⁴ Ram was the father of Amminadab.

Amminadab was the father of Nahshon.

Nahshon was the father of Salmon.

⁵ Salmon was the father of Boaz (his mother was Rahab).

Boaz was the father of Obed (his mother was Ruth).

Obed was the father of Jesse.

⁶ Jesse was the father of King David.

David was the father of Solomon (his mother was Bathsheba, the widow of Uriah).

⁷ Solomon was the father of Rehoboam.

Rehoboam was the father of Abijah.

Abijah was the father of Asaph.*

⁸ Asaph was the father of Jehoshaphat.

Jehoshaphat was the father of Jehoram.*ª

Jehoram was the father*ᵇ of Uzziah.

⁹ Uzziah was the father of Jotham.

Jotham was the father of Ahaz.

Ahaz was the father of Hezekiah.

¹⁰ Hezekiah was the father of Manasseh.

Manasseh was the father of Amos.*

Amos was the father of Josiah.

[11] Josiah was the father of Jehoiachin* and his brothers (born at the time of the exile to Babylon).

[12] After the Babylonian exile:

Jehoiachin was the father of Shealtiel.

Shealtiel was the father of Zerubbabel.

[13] Zerubbabel was the father of Abiud.

Abiud was the father of Eliakim.

Eliakim was the father of Azor.

[14] Azor was the father of Zadok.

Zadok was the father of Akim.

Akim was the father of Eliud.

[15] Eliud was the father of Eleazar.

Eleazar was the father of Matthan.

Matthan was the father of Jacob.

[16] Jacob was the father of Joseph, the husband of Mary.

Mary was the mother of Jesus, who is called the Messiah.

[17] All those listed above include fourteen generations from Abraham to King David, and fourteen from David's time to the Babylonian exile, and fourteen from the Babylonian exile to the Messiah.

The Birth of Jesus the Messiah

[18] Now this is how Jesus the Messiah was born. His mother, Mary, was engaged to be married to Joseph. But while she was still a virgin, she became pregnant by the Holy Spirit. [19] Joseph, her fiancé, being a just man, decided to break the engagement quietly, so as not to disgrace her publicly.

[20] As he considered this, he fell asleep, and an angel of the Lord appeared to him in a dream. "Joseph, son of David," the angel said, "do not be afraid to go ahead with your marriage to Mary. For the child within her has been

conceived by the Holy Spirit. [21] And she will have a son, and you are to name him Jesus,* for he will save his people from their sins." [22] All of this happened to fulfil the Lord's message through his prophet:

[23] "Look! The virgin will conceive a child!
    She will give birth to a son,
  and he will be called Immanuel*
    (meaning, God is with us)."

[24] When Joseph woke up, he did what the angel of the Lord commanded. He brought Mary home to be his wife, [25] but she remained a virgin until her son was born. And Joseph named him Jesus.

CHAPTER 2

The Visit of the Wise Men

Jesus was born in the town of Bethlehem in Judea, during the reign of King Herod. About that time some wise men* from eastern lands arrived in Jerusalem, asking, [2] "Where is the newborn king of the Jews? We have seen his star as it arose,* and we have come to worship him."

[3] Herod was deeply disturbed by their question, as was all of Jerusalem. [4] He called a meeting of the leading priests and teachers of religious law. "Where did the prophets say the Messiah would be born?" he asked them.

[5] "In Bethlehem," they said, "for this is what the prophet wrote:

[6] 'O Bethlehem of Judah,
    you are not just a lowly village in Judah,
  for a ruler will come from you
    who will be the shepherd for my people Israel.'* "

[7] Then Herod sent a private message to the wise men, asking them to come and see him. At this meeting he learned the exact time when they first saw the star. [8] Then he told them, "Go to Bethlehem and search carefully for the child. And when you find him, come back and tell me so that I can go and worship him, too!"

[9] After this interview the wise men went their way. Once again the star appeared to them, guiding them to Bethlehem. It went ahead of them and stopped over the place where the child was. [10] When they saw the star, they were filled with joy! [11] They entered the house where the child and his mother, Mary, were, and they fell down before him and worshipped him. Then they opened their treasure chests and gave him gifts of gold, frankincense, and myrrh. [12] But when it was time to leave, they went home another way, because God had warned them in a dream not to return to Herod.

The Escape to Egypt

[13] After the wise men had gone, an angel of the Lord appeared to Joseph in a dream. "Get up and flee to Egypt with the child and his mother," the angel said. "Stay there until I tell you to return, because Herod is going to try to kill the child." [14] That night Joseph left for Egypt with the child and Mary, his mother, [15] and they stayed there until Herod's death. This fulfilled what the Lord had spoken through the prophet: "I called my Son out of Egypt."*

[16] Herod was furious when he learned that the wise men had outwitted him. He sent soldiers to kill all the boys in and around Bethlehem who were two years old and under, because the wise men had told him that the star first

appeared to them about two years earlier.* ¹⁷Herod's brutal action fulfilled the prophecy of Jeremiah:
¹⁸"A cry of anguish is heard in Ramah—
    weeping and mourning unrestrained.
Rachel weeps for her children,
    refusing to be comforted—for they are dead."*

The Return to Nazareth

¹⁹When Herod died, an angel of the Lord appeared in a dream to Joseph in Egypt and told him, ²⁰"Get up and take the child and his mother back to the land of Israel, because those who were trying to kill the child are dead." ²¹So Joseph returned immediately to Israel with Jesus and his mother. ²²But when he learned that the new ruler was Herod's son Archelaus, he was afraid. Then, in another dream, he was warned to go to Galilee. ²³So they went and lived in a town called Nazareth. This fulfilled what was spoken by the prophets concerning the Messiah: "He will be called a Nazarene."

CHAPTER 3

John the Baptist Prepares the Way

In those days John the Baptist began preaching in the Judean wilderness. His message was, ²"Turn from your sins and turn to God, because the Kingdom of Heaven is near."* ³Isaiah had spoken of John when he said,
    "He is a voice shouting in the wilderness:
    'Prepare a pathway for the Lord's coming!
        Make a straight road for him!'"*
⁴John's clothes were woven from camel hair, and he wore a leather belt; his food was locusts and wild honey. ⁵People

from Jerusalem and from every section of Judea and from all over the Jordan Valley went out to the wilderness to hear him preach. ⁶And when they confessed their sins, he baptized them in the River Jordan.

⁷But when he saw many Pharisees and Sadducees coming to be baptized, he denounced them. "You brood of snakes!" he exclaimed. "Who warned you to flee God's coming judgement? ⁸Prove by the way you live that you have really turned from your sins and turned to God. ⁹Don't just say, 'We're safe—we're the descendants of Abraham.' That proves nothing. God can change these stones here into children of Abraham. ¹⁰Even now the axe of God's judgement is poised, ready to sever your roots. Yes, every tree that does not produce good fruit will be chopped down and thrown into the fire.

¹¹"I baptize with*ᵃ water those who turn from their sins and turn to God. But someone is coming soon who is far greater than I am—so much greater that I am not even worthy to be his slave.*ᵇ He will baptize you with the Holy Spirit and with fire.*ᶜ ¹²He is ready to separate the chaff from the grain with his winnowing fork. Then he will clean up the threshing area, storing the grain in his barn but burning the chaff with never-ending fire."

The Baptism of Jesus

¹³Then Jesus went from Galilee to the River Jordan to be baptized by John. ¹⁴But John didn't want to baptize him. "I am the one who needs to be baptized by you," he said, "so why are you coming to me?"

¹⁵But Jesus said, "It must be done, because we must do everything that is right." So then John baptized him.

[16] After his baptism, as Jesus came up out of the water, the heavens were opened and he saw the Spirit of God descending like a dove and settling on him. [17] And a voice from heaven said, "This is my beloved Son, and I am fully pleased with him."

CHAPTER 4

The Temptation of Jesus

Then Jesus was led out into the wilderness by the Holy Spirit to be tempted there by the Devil. [2] For forty days and forty nights he ate nothing and became very hungry. [3] Then the Devil* came and said to him, "If you are the Son of God, change these stones into loaves of bread."

[4] But Jesus told him, "No! The Scriptures say,

'People need more than bread for their life;
    they must feed on every word of God.'* "

[5] Then the Devil took him to Jerusalem, to the highest point of the Temple, [6] and said, "If you are the Son of God, jump off! For the Scriptures say,

'He orders his angels to protect you.
And they will hold you with their hands
    to keep you from striking your foot on a stone.'* "

[7] Jesus responded, "The Scriptures also say, 'Do not test the Lord your God.'* "

[8] Next the Devil took him to the peak of a very high mountain and showed him the nations of the world and all their glory. [9] "I will give it all to you," he said, "if you will only kneel down and worship me."

[10] "Get out of here, Satan," Jesus told him. "For the Scriptures say,

'You must worship the Lord your God;

serve only him."* "

[11] Then the Devil went away, and angels came and cared for Jesus.

The Ministry of Jesus Begins

[12] When Jesus heard that John had been arrested, he left Judea and returned to Galilee. [13] But instead of going to Nazareth, he went to Capernaum, beside the Sea of Galilee, in the region of Zebulun and Naphtali. [14] This fulfilled Isaiah's prophecy:

[15] "In the land of Zebulun and of Naphtali,
　　beside the sea, beyond the River Jordan—
　　in Galilee where so many Gentiles live—
[16] the people who sat in darkness
　　have seen a great light.
And for those who lived in the land where death casts its
　　　　shadow,
　　a light has shined."*

[17] From then on, Jesus began to preach, "Turn from your sins and turn to God, because the Kingdom of Heaven is near.*"

The First Disciples

[18] One day as Jesus was walking along the shore beside the Sea of Galilee, he saw two brothers—Simon, also called Peter, and Andrew—fishing with a net, for they were commercial fishermen. [19] Jesus called out to them, "Come, be my disciples, and I will show you how to fish for people!" [20] And they left their nets at once and went with him.

[21] A little farther up the shore he saw two other brothers, James and John, sitting in a boat with their father, Zebedee, mending their nets. And he called them to come,

too. ²²They immediately followed him, leaving the boat and their father behind.

The Ministry of Jesus in Galilee

²³Jesus travelled throughout Galilee teaching in the synagogues, preaching everywhere the Good News about the Kingdom. And he healed people who had every kind of sickness and disease. ²⁴News about him spread far beyond the borders of Galilee so that the sick were soon coming to be healed from as far away as Syria. And whatever their illness and pain, or whether they were possessed by demons, or were epileptics, or were paralysed—he healed them all. ²⁵Large crowds followed him wherever he went—people from Galilee, the Ten Towns,* Jerusalem, from all over Judea, and from east of the River Jordan.

CHAPTER 5

The Sermon on the Mount

One day as the crowds were gathering, Jesus went up the mountainside with his disciples and sat down to teach them.

The Beatitudes

²This is what he taught them:
³ "God blesses those who realize their need for him,*
    for the Kingdom of Heaven is given to them.
⁴ God blesses those who mourn,
    for they will be comforted.
⁵ God blesses those who are gentle and lowly,
    for the whole earth will belong to them.
⁶ God blesses those who are hungry and thirsty for justice,
    for they will receive it in full.

⁷ God blesses those who are merciful,
  for they will be shown mercy.

⁸ God blesses those whose hearts are pure,
  for they will see God.

⁹ God blesses those who work for peace,
  for they will be called the children of God.

¹⁰ God blesses those who are persecuted because they live
    for God,
  for the Kingdom of Heaven is theirs.

¹¹ "God blesses you when you are mocked and persecuted and lied about because you are my followers. ¹²Be happy about it! Be very glad! For a great reward awaits you in heaven. And remember, the ancient prophets were persecuted, too.

Teaching about Salt and Light

¹³ "You are the salt of the earth. But what good is salt if it has lost its flavour? Can you make it useful again? It will be thrown out and trampled underfoot as worthless. ¹⁴You are the light of the world—like a city on a mountain, glowing in the night for all to see. ¹⁵Don't hide your light under a basket! Instead, put it on a stand and let it shine for all. ¹⁶In the same way, let your good deeds shine out for all to see, so that everyone will praise your heavenly Father.

Teaching about the Law

¹⁷ "Don't misunderstand why I have come. I did not come to abolish the law of Moses or the writings of the prophets. No, I came to fulfil them. ¹⁸I assure you, until heaven and earth disappear, even the smallest detail of God's law will remain until its purpose is achieved. ¹⁹So if you break the smallest commandment and teach others to do the same,

you will be the least in the Kingdom of Heaven. But anyone who obeys God's laws and teaches them will be great in the Kingdom of Heaven.

²⁰ "But I warn you—unless you obey God better than the teachers of religious law and the Pharisees do, you can't enter the Kingdom of Heaven at all!

Teaching about Anger

²¹ "You have heard that the law of Moses says, 'Do not murder. If you commit murder, you are subject to judgement.'* ²² But I say, if you are angry with someone,*ª you are subject to judgement! If you call someone an idiot,*ᵇ you are in danger of being brought before the high council. And if you curse someone,*ᶜ you are in danger of the fires of hell.

²³ "So if you are standing before the altar in the Temple, offering a sacrifice to God, and you suddenly remember that someone has something against you, ²⁴ leave your sacrifice there beside the altar. Go and be reconciled to that person. Then come and offer your sacrifice to God. ²⁵ Come to terms quickly with your enemy before it is too late and you are dragged into court, handed over to an officer, and thrown in jail. ²⁶ I assure you that you won't be free again until you have paid the last penny.

Teaching about Adultery

²⁷ "You have heard that the law of Moses says, 'Do not commit adultery.'* ²⁸ But I say, anyone who even looks at a woman with lust in his eye has already committed adultery with her in his heart. ²⁹ So if your eye—even if it is your good eye*—causes you to lust, gouge it out and throw it away. It is better for you to lose one part of your body than

for your whole body to be thrown into hell. ³⁰ And if your hand—even if it is your stronger hand*—causes you to sin, cut it off and throw it away. It is better for you to lose one part of your body than for your whole body to be thrown into hell.

Teaching about Divorce

³¹ "You have heard that the law of Moses says, 'A man can divorce his wife by merely giving her a letter of divorce.'* ³² But I say that a man who divorces his wife, unless she has been unfaithful, causes her to commit adultery. And anyone who marries a divorced woman commits adultery.

Teaching about Vows

³³ "Again, you have heard that the law of Moses says, 'Do not break your vows; you must carry out the vows you have made to the Lord.'* ³⁴ But I say, don't make any vows! If you say, 'By heaven!' it is a sacred vow because heaven is God's throne. ³⁵ And if you say, 'By the earth!' it is a sacred vow because the earth is his footstool. And don't swear, 'By Jerusalem!' for Jerusalem is the city of the great King. ³⁶ Don't even swear, 'By my head!' for you can't turn one hair white or black. ³⁷ Just say a simple, 'Yes, I will,' or 'No, I won't.' Your word is enough. To strengthen your promise with a vow shows that something is wrong.*

Teaching about Revenge

³⁸ "You have heard that the law of Moses says, 'If an eye is injured, injure the eye of the person who did it. If a tooth gets knocked out, knock out the tooth of the person who did it.'* ³⁹ But I say, don't resist an evil person! If you are slapped on the right cheek, turn the other, too. ⁴⁰ If you are

ordered to court and your shirt is taken from you, give your coat, too. ⁴¹If a soldier demands that you carry his gear for a kilometre,* carry it two kilometres. ⁴²Give to those who ask, and don't turn away from those who want to borrow.

Teaching about Love for Enemies

⁴³"You have heard that the law of Moses says, 'Love your neighbour'* and hate your enemy. ⁴⁴But I say, love your enemies!* Pray for those who persecute you! ⁴⁵In that way, you will be acting as true children of your Father in heaven. For he gives his sunlight to both the evil and the good, and he sends rain on the just and on the unjust, too. ⁴⁶If you love only those who love you, what good is that? Even corrupt tax collectors do that much. ⁴⁷If you are kind only to your friends,* how are you different from anyone else? Even pagans do that. ⁴⁸But you are to be perfect, even as your Father in heaven is perfect.

CHAPTER 6

Teaching about Giving to the Needy

"Take care! Don't do your good deeds publicly, to be admired, because then you will lose the reward from your Father in heaven. ²When you give a gift to someone in need, don't shout about it as the hypocrites do—blowing trumpets in the synagogues and streets to call attention to their acts of charity! I assure you, they have received all the reward they will ever get. ³But when you give to someone, don't tell your left hand what your right hand is doing. ⁴Give your gifts in secret, and your Father, who knows all secrets, will reward you.

Teaching about Prayer and Fasting

[5] "And now about prayer. When you pray, don't be like the hypocrites who love to pray publicly on street corners and in the synagogues where everyone can see them. I assure you, that is all the reward they will ever get. [6] But when you pray, go away by yourself, shut the door behind you, and pray to your Father secretly. Then your Father, who knows all secrets, will reward you.

[7] "When you pray, don't babble on and on as people of other religions do. They think their prayers are answered only by repeating their words again and again. [8] Don't be like them, because your Father knows exactly what you need even before you ask him! [9] Pray like this:

Our Father in heaven,
    may your name be honoured.
[10] May your Kingdom come soon.
May your will be done here on earth,
    just as it is in heaven.
[11] Give us our food for today,*
[12] and forgive us our sins,
    just as we have forgiven those who have sinned
        against us.
[13] And don't let us yield to temptation,
    but deliver us from the evil one.*

[14] "If you forgive those who sin against you, your heavenly Father will forgive you. [15] But if you refuse to forgive others, your Father will not forgive your sins.

[16] "And when you fast, don't make it obvious, as the hypocrites do, who try to look pale and dishevelled so people will admire them for their fasting. I assure you, that is the only reward they will ever get. [17] But when you fast, comb your hair and wash your face. [18] Then no one will

suspect you are fasting, except your Father, who knows what you do in secret. And your Father, who knows all secrets, will reward you.

Teaching about Money and Possessions

19 "Don't store up treasures here on earth, where they can be eaten by moths and get rusty, and where thieves break in and steal. 20 Store your treasures in heaven, where they will never become moth-eaten or rusty and where they will be safe from thieves. 21 Wherever your treasure is, there your heart and thoughts will also be.

22 "Your eye is a lamp for your body. A pure eye lets sunshine into your soul. 23 But an evil eye shuts out the light and plunges you into darkness. If the light you think you have is really darkness, how deep that darkness will be!

24 "No one can serve two masters. For you will hate one and love the other, or be devoted to one and despise the other. You cannot serve both God and money.

25 "So I tell you, don't worry about everyday life—whether you have enough food, drink, and clothes. Doesn't life consist of more than food and clothing? 26 Look at the birds. They don't need to plant or harvest or put food in barns, for your heavenly Father feeds them. And you are far more valuable to him than they are. 27 Can all your worries add a single moment to your life? Of course not.

28 "And why worry about your clothes? Look at the lilies and how they grow. They don't work or make their clothing, 29 yet Solomon in all his glory was not dressed as beautifully as they are. 30 And if God cares so wonderfully for flowers that are here today and gone tomorrow, won't he more surely care for you? You have so little faith!

[31] "So don't worry about having enough food or drink or clothing. [32] Why be like the pagans who are so deeply concerned about these things? Your heavenly Father already knows all your needs, [33] and he will give you all you need from day to day if you live for him and make the Kingdom of God your primary concern.

[34] "So don't worry about tomorrow, for tomorrow will bring its own worries. Today's trouble is enough for today.

CHAPTER 7

Don't Condemn Others

"Stop judging others, and you will not be judged. [2] For others will treat you as you treat them.* Whatever measure you use in judging others, it will be used to measure how you are judged. [3] And why worry about a speck in your friend's eye* when you have a log in your own? [4] How can you think of saying, 'Let me help you get rid of that speck in your eye,' when you can't see past the log in your own eye? [5] Hypocrite! First get rid of the log from your own eye; then perhaps you will see well enough to deal with the speck in your friend's eye.

[6] "Don't give what is holy to unholy people.* Don't give pearls to swine! They will trample the pearls, then turn and attack you.

Effective Prayer

[7] "Keep on asking, and you will be given what you ask for. Keep on looking, and you will find. Keep on knocking, and the door will be opened. [8] For everyone who asks, receives. Everyone who seeks, finds. And the door is opened to everyone who knocks. [9] You parents—if your children ask for

a loaf of bread, do you give them a stone instead? ¹⁰ Or if they ask for a fish, do you give them a snake? Of course not! ¹¹ If you sinful people know how to give good gifts to your children, how much more will your heavenly Father give good gifts to those who ask him.

The Golden Rule

¹² "Do for others what you would like them to do for you. This is a summary of all that is taught in the law and the prophets.

The Narrow Gate

¹³ "You can enter God's Kingdom only through the narrow gate. The highway to hell* is broad, and its gate is wide for the many who choose the easy way. ¹⁴ But the gateway to life is small, and the road is narrow, and only a few ever find it.

The Tree and Its Fruit

¹⁵ "Beware of false prophets who come disguised as harmless sheep, but are really wolves that will tear you apart. ¹⁶ You can detect them by the way they act, just as you can identify a tree by its fruit. You don't pick grapes from thorn bushes, or figs from thistles. ¹⁷ A healthy tree produces good fruit, and an unhealthy tree produces bad fruit. ¹⁸ A good tree can't produce bad fruit, and a bad tree can't produce good fruit. ¹⁹ So every tree that does not produce good fruit is chopped down and thrown into the fire. ²⁰ Yes, the way to identify a tree or a person is by the kind of fruit that is produced.

True Disciples

²¹ "Not all people who sound religious are really godly. They may refer to me as 'Lord,' but they still won't enter the

Kingdom of Heaven. The decisive issue is whether they obey my Father in heaven. ²²On judgement day many will tell me, 'Lord, Lord, we prophesied in your name and cast out demons in your name and performed many miracles in your name.' ²³But I will reply, 'I never knew you. Go away; the things you did were unauthorized.'"

Building on a Solid Foundation

²⁴"Anyone who listens to my teaching and obeys me is wise, like a person who builds a house on solid rock. ²⁵Though the rain comes in torrents and the floodwaters rise and the winds beat against that house, it won't collapse, because it is built on rock. ²⁶But anyone who hears my teaching and ignores it is foolish, like a person who builds a house on sand. ²⁷When the rains and floods come and the winds beat against that house, it will fall with a mighty crash."

²⁸After Jesus finished speaking, the crowds were amazed at his teaching, ²⁹for he taught as one who had real authority—quite unlike the teachers of religious law.

CHAPTER 8

Jesus Heals a Man with Leprosy

Large crowds followed Jesus as he came down the mountainside. ²Suddenly, a man with leprosy approached Jesus. He knelt before him, worshipping. "Lord," the man said, "if you want to, you can make me well again."

³Jesus touched him. "I want to," he said. "Be healed!" And instantly the leprosy disappeared. ⁴Then Jesus said to him, "Go straight over to the priest and let him examine you. Don't talk to anyone along the way. Take along the offering required in the law of Moses for those who have been

healed of leprosy, so everyone will have proof of your healing."

Faith of the Roman Officer

[5]When Jesus arrived in Capernaum, a Roman officer came and pleaded with him, [6]"Lord, my young servant lies in bed, paralysed and racked with pain."

[7]Jesus said, "I will come and heal him."

[8]Then the officer said, "Lord, I am not worthy to have you come into my home. Just say the word from where you are, and my servant will be healed! [9]I know, because I am under the authority of my superior officers and I have authority over my soldiers. I only need to say, 'Go,' and they go, or 'Come,' and they come. And if I say to my slaves, 'Do this or that,' they do it."

[10]When Jesus heard this, he was amazed. Turning to the crowd, he said, "I tell you the truth, I haven't seen faith like this in all the land of Israel! [11]And I tell you this, that many Gentiles will come from all over the world and sit down with Abraham, Isaac, and Jacob at the feast in the Kingdom of Heaven. [12]But many Israelites—those for whom the Kingdom was prepared—will be cast into outer darkness, where there will be weeping and gnashing of teeth."

[13]Then Jesus said to the Roman officer, "Go on home. What you have believed has happened." And the young servant was healed that same hour.

Jesus Heals Many People

[14]When Jesus arrived at Peter's house, Peter's mother-in-law was in bed with a high fever. [15]But when Jesus touched her hand, the fever left her. Then she got up and prepared a meal for him.

[16]That evening many demon-possessed people were brought to Jesus. All the spirits fled when he commanded them to leave; and he healed all the sick. [17]This fulfilled the word of the Lord through Isaiah, who said, "He took our sicknesses and removed our diseases."*

The Cost of Following Jesus

[18]When Jesus noticed how large the crowd was growing, he instructed his disciples to cross to the other side of the lake.

[19]Then one of the teachers of religious law said to him, "Teacher, I will follow you no matter where you go!"

[20]But Jesus said, "Foxes have dens to live in, and birds have nests, but I, the Son of Man, have no home of my own, not even a place to lay my head."

[21]Another of his disciples said, "Lord, first let me return home and bury my father."

[22]But Jesus told him, "Follow me now! Let those who are spiritually dead care for their own dead."*

Jesus Calms the Storm

[23]Then Jesus got into the boat and started across the lake with his disciples. [24]Suddenly, a terrible storm came up, with waves breaking into the boat. But Jesus was sleeping. [25]The disciples went to him and woke him up, shouting, "Lord, save us! We're going to drown!"

[26]And Jesus answered, "Why are you afraid? You have so little faith!" Then he stood up and rebuked the wind and waves, and suddenly all was calm. [27]The disciples just sat there in awe. "Who is this?" they asked themselves. "Even the wind and waves obey him!"

Jesus Heals Two Demon-Possessed Men

[28] When Jesus arrived on the other side of the lake in the land of the Gadarenes,* two men who were possessed by demons met him. They lived in a cemetery and were so dangerous that no one could go through that area. [29] They began screaming at him, "Why are you bothering us, Son of God? You have no right to torture us before God's appointed time!" [30] A large herd of pigs was feeding in the distance, [31] so the demons begged, "If you cast us out, send us into that herd of pigs."

[32] "All right, go!" Jesus commanded them. So the demons came out of the men and entered the pigs, and the whole herd plunged down the steep hillside into the lake and drowned in the water. [33] The herdsmen fled to the nearby city, telling everyone what happened to the demon-possessed men. [34] The entire town came out to meet Jesus, but they begged him to go away and leave them alone.

CHAPTER 9

Jesus Heals a Paralysed Man

Jesus climbed into a boat and went back across the lake to his own town. [2] Some people brought to him a paralysed man on a mat. Seeing their faith, Jesus said to the paralysed man, "Take heart, my child! Your sins are forgiven."

[3] "Blasphemy! This man talks as if he were God!" some of the teachers of religious law said among themselves.

[4] Jesus knew what they were thinking, so he asked them, "Why are you thinking such evil thoughts? [5] Is it easier to say, 'Your sins are forgiven' or 'Get up and walk'? [6] I will prove that I, the Son of Man, have the authority on earth

to forgive sins." Then Jesus turned to the paralysed man and said, "Stand up, take your mat, and go on home, because you are healed!"

⁷And the man jumped up and went home! ⁸Fear swept through the crowd as they saw this happen right before their eyes. They praised God for sending a man with such great authority.

Jesus Calls Matthew

⁹As Jesus was going down the road, he saw Matthew sitting at his tax-collection booth. "Come, be my disciple," Jesus said to him. So Matthew got up and followed him.

¹⁰That night Matthew invited Jesus and his disciples to be his dinner guests, along with his fellow tax collectors and many other notorious sinners. ¹¹The Pharisees were indignant. "Why does your teacher eat with such scum*?" they asked his disciples.

¹²When he heard this, Jesus replied, "Healthy people don't need a doctor—sick people do." ¹³Then he added, "Now go and learn the meaning of this Scripture: 'I want you to be merciful; I don't want your sacrifices.'* For I have come to call sinners, not those who think they are already good enough."

A Discussion about Fasting

¹⁴One day the disciples of John the Baptist came to Jesus and asked him, "Why do we and the Pharisees fast, but your disciples don't fast?"

¹⁵Jesus responded, "Should the wedding guests mourn while celebrating with the groom? Someday he will be taken from them, and then they will fast. ¹⁶And who would patch an old garment with unshrunk cloth? For the patch

shrinks and pulls away from the old cloth, leaving an even bigger hole than before. [17] And no one puts new wine into old wineskins. The old skins would burst from the pressure, spilling the wine and ruining the skins. New wine must be stored in new wineskins. That way both the wine and the wineskins are preserved."

Jesus Heals in Response to Faith

[18] As Jesus was saying this, the leader of a synagogue came and knelt down before him. "My daughter has just died," he said, "but you can bring her back to life again if you just come and lay your hand upon her."

[19] As Jesus and the disciples were going to the official's home, [20] a woman who had had a haemorrhage for twelve years came up behind him. She touched the fringe of his robe, [21] for she thought, "If I can just touch his robe, I will be healed."

[22] Jesus turned around and said to her, "Daughter, be encouraged! Your faith has made you well." And the woman was healed at that moment.

[23] When Jesus arrived at the official's home, he noticed the noisy crowds and heard the funeral music. [24] He said, "Go away, for the girl isn't dead; she's only asleep." But the crowd laughed at him. [25] When the crowd was finally outside, Jesus went in and took the girl by the hand, and she stood up! [26] The report of this miracle swept through the entire countryside.

Jesus Heals the Blind and Mute

[27] After Jesus left the girl's home, two blind men followed along behind him, shouting, "Son of David, have mercy on us!"

[28] They went right into the house where he was staying, and Jesus asked them, "Do you believe I can make you see?"

"Yes, Lord," they told him, "we do."

[29] Then he touched their eyes and said, "Because of your faith, it will happen." [30] And suddenly they could see! Jesus sternly warned them, "Don't tell anyone about this." [31] But instead, they spread his fame all over the region.

[32] When they left, some people brought to him a man who couldn't speak because he was possessed by a demon. [33] So Jesus cast out the demon, and instantly the man could talk. The crowds marvelled. "Nothing like this has ever happened in Israel!" they exclaimed.

[34] But the Pharisees said, "He can cast out demons because he is empowered by the prince of demons."

The Need for Workers

[35] Jesus travelled through all the cities and villages of that area, teaching in the synagogues and announcing the Good News about the Kingdom. And wherever he went, he healed people of every sort of disease and illness. [36] He felt great pity for the crowds that came, because their problems were so great and they didn't know where to go for help. They were like sheep without a shepherd. [37] He said to his disciples, "The harvest is so great, but the workers are so few. [38] So pray to the Lord who is in charge of the harvest; ask him to send out more workers for his fields."

CHAPTER 10

Jesus Sends Out the Twelve Apostles

Jesus called his twelve disciples to him and gave them authority to cast out evil spirits and to heal every kind of disease and illness. ²Here are the names of the twelve apostles:

first Simon (also called Peter),
  then Andrew (Peter's brother),
  James (son of Zebedee),
  John (James's brother),
³ Philip,
  Bartholomew,
  Thomas,
  Matthew (the tax collector),
  James (son of Alphaeus),
  Thaddaeus,
⁴ Simon (the Zealot*),
  Judas Iscariot (who later betrayed him).

⁵Jesus sent the twelve disciples out with these instructions: "Don't go to the Gentiles or the Samaritans, ⁶but only to the people of Israel—God's lost sheep. ⁷Go and announce to them that the Kingdom of Heaven is near.* ⁸Heal the sick, raise the dead, cure those with leprosy, and cast out demons. Give as freely as you have received!

⁹"Don't take any money with you. ¹⁰Don't carry a traveller's bag with an extra coat and sandals or even a walking stick. Don't hesitate to accept hospitality, because those who work deserve to be fed.* ¹¹Whenever you enter a city or village, search for a worthy man and stay in his home until you leave for the next town. ¹²When you are invited into someone's home, give it your blessing. ¹³If it turns out to be a worthy home, let your blessing stand; if it is not, take back the blessing. ¹⁴If a village doesn't welcome you or listen to you, shake off the dust of that place from your feet as you leave. ¹⁵I assure you, the wicked cities of

Sodom and Gomorrah will be better off on the judgement day than that place will be.

¹⁶ "Look, I am sending you out as sheep among wolves. Be as wary as snakes and harmless as doves. ¹⁷ But beware! For you will be handed over to the courts and beaten in the synagogues. ¹⁸ And you must stand trial before governors and kings because you are my followers. This will be your opportunity to tell them about me—yes, to witness to the world. ¹⁹ When you are arrested, don't worry about what to say in your defence, because you will be given the right words at the right time. ²⁰ For it won't be you doing the talking—it will be the Spirit of your Father speaking through you.

²¹ "Brother will betray brother to death, fathers will betray their own children, and children will rise against their parents and cause them to be killed. ²² And everyone will hate you because of your allegiance to me. But those who endure to the end will be saved. ²³ When you are persecuted in one town, flee to the next. I assure you that I, the Son of Man, will return before you have reached all the towns of Israel.

²⁴ "A student is not greater than the teacher. A servant is not greater than the master. ²⁵ The student shares the teacher's fate. The servant shares the master's fate. And since I, the master of the household, have been called the prince of demons,* how much more will it happen to you, the members of the household! ²⁶ But don't be afraid of those who threaten you. For the time is coming when everything will be revealed; all that is secret will be made public. ²⁷ What I tell you now in the darkness, shout abroad when daybreak comes. What I whisper in your ears, shout from the housetops for all to hear!

²⁸"Don't be afraid of those who want to kill you. They can only kill your body; they cannot touch your soul. Fear only God, who can destroy both soul and body in hell. ²⁹Not even a sparrow, worth only half a penny, can fall to the ground without your Father knowing it. ³⁰And the very hairs on your head are all numbered. ³¹So don't be afraid; you are more valuable to him than a whole flock of sparrows.

³²"If anyone acknowledges me publicly here on earth, I will openly acknowledge that person before my Father in heaven. ³³But if anyone denies me here on earth, I will deny that person before my Father in heaven.

³⁴"Don't imagine that I came to bring peace to the earth! No, I came to bring a sword. ³⁵I have come to set a man against his father, and a daughter against her mother, and a daughter-in-law against her mother-in-law. ³⁶Your enemies will be right in your own household! ³⁷If you love your father or mother more than you love me, you are not worthy of being mine; or if you love your son or daughter more than me, you are not worthy of being mine. ³⁸If you refuse to take up your cross and follow me, you are not worthy of being mine. ³⁹If you cling to your life, you will lose it; but if you give it up for me, you will find it.

⁴⁰"Anyone who welcomes you is welcoming me, and anyone who welcomes me is welcoming the Father who sent me. ⁴¹If you welcome a prophet as one who speaks for God,* you will receive the same reward a prophet gets. And if you welcome good and godly people because of their godliness, you will be given a reward like theirs. ⁴²And if you give even a cup of cold water to one of the least of my followers, you will surely be rewarded."

CHAPTER 11

Jesus and John the Baptist

When Jesus had finished giving these instructions to his twelve disciples, he went off teaching and preaching in towns throughout the country.

² John the Baptist, who was now in prison, heard about all the things the Messiah was doing. So he sent his disciples to ask Jesus, ³ "Are you really the Messiah we've been waiting for, or should we keep looking for someone else?"

⁴ Jesus told them, "Go back to John and tell him about what you have heard and seen—⁵ the blind see, the lame walk, the lepers are cured, the deaf hear, the dead are raised to life, and the Good News is being preached to the poor. ⁶ And tell him: 'God blesses those who are not offended by me.*'"

⁷ When John's disciples had gone, Jesus began talking about him to the crowds. "Who is this man in the wilderness that you went out to see? Did you find him weak as a reed, moved by every breath of wind? ⁸ Or were you expecting to see a man dressed in expensive clothes? Those who dress like that live in palaces, not out in the wilderness. ⁹ Were you looking for a prophet? Yes, and he is more than a prophet. ¹⁰ John is the man to whom the Scriptures refer when they say,

'Look, I am sending my messenger before you,
    and he will prepare your way before you.'*

¹¹ "I assure you, of all who have ever lived, none is greater than John the Baptist. Yet even the most insignificant person in the Kingdom of Heaven is greater than he is! ¹² And from the time John the Baptist began preaching and baptizing until now, the Kingdom of Heaven has been

forcefully advancing, and violent people attack it.* ¹³ For before John came, all the teachings of the Scriptures looked forward to this present time. ¹⁴ And if you are willing to accept what I say, he is Elijah, the one the prophets said would come.* ¹⁵ Anyone who is willing to hear should listen and understand!

¹⁶ "How shall I describe this generation? These people are like a group of children playing a game in the public square. They complain to their friends, ¹⁷ 'We played wedding songs, and you weren't happy, so we played funeral songs, but you weren't sad.' ¹⁸ For John the Baptist didn't drink wine and he often fasted, and you say, 'He's demon-possessed.' ¹⁹ And I, the Son of Man, feast and drink, and you say, 'He's a glutton and a drunkard, and a friend of the worst sort of sinners!' But wisdom is shown to be right by what results from it."

Judgement for the Unbelievers

²⁰ Then Jesus began to denounce the cities where he had done most of his miracles, because they hadn't turned from their sins and turned to God. ²¹ "What horrors await you, Korazin and Bethsaida! For if the miracles I did in you had been done in wicked Tyre and Sidon, their people would have sat in deep repentance long ago, clothed in sackcloth and throwing ashes on their heads to show their remorse. ²² I assure you, Tyre and Sidon will be better off on the judgement day than you! ²³ And you people of Capernaum, will you be exalted to heaven? No, you will be brought down to the place of the dead.* For if the miracles I did for you had been done in Sodom, it would still be here today. ²⁴ I assure you, Sodom will be better off on the judgement day than you."

Jesus' Prayer of Thanksgiving

[25] Then Jesus prayed this prayer: "O Father, Lord of heaven and earth, thank you for hiding the truth from those who think themselves so wise and clever, and for revealing it to the childlike. [26] Yes, Father, it pleased you to do it this way!

[27] "My Father has given me authority over everything. No one really knows the Son except the Father, and no one really knows the Father except the Son and those to whom the Son chooses to reveal him."

[28] Then Jesus said, "Come to me, all of you who are weary and carry heavy burdens, and I will give you rest. [29] Take my yoke upon you. Let me teach you, because I am humble and gentle, and you will find rest for your souls. [30] For my yoke fits perfectly, and the burden I give you is light."

CHAPTER 12

Controversy about the Sabbath

At about that time Jesus was walking through some cornfields on the Sabbath. His disciples were hungry, so they began breaking off heads of wheat and eating the grain. [2] Some Pharisees saw them do it and protested, "Your disciples shouldn't be doing that! It's against the law to work by harvesting corn on the Sabbath."

[3] But Jesus said to them, "Haven't you ever read in the Scriptures what King David did when he and his companions were hungry? [4] He went into the house of God, and they ate the special bread reserved for the priests alone. That was breaking the law, too. [5] And haven't you ever read in the law of Moses that the priests on duty in the Temple may work on the Sabbath? [6] I tell you, there is

one here who is even greater than the Temple! ⁷But you would not have condemned those who aren't guilty if you knew the meaning of this Scripture: 'I want you to be merciful; I don't want your sacrifices.'* ⁸For I, the Son of Man, am master even of the Sabbath."

⁹Then he went over to the synagogue, ¹⁰where he noticed a man with a deformed hand. The Pharisees asked Jesus, "Is it legal to work by healing on the Sabbath day?" (They were, of course, hoping he would say yes, so they could bring charges against him.)

¹¹And he answered, "If you had one sheep, and it fell into a well on the Sabbath, wouldn't you get to work and pull it out? Of course you would. ¹²And how much more valuable is a person than a sheep! Yes, it is right to do good on the Sabbath." ¹³Then he said to the man, "Reach out your hand." The man reached out his hand, and it became normal, just like the other one. ¹⁴Then the Pharisees called a meeting and discussed plans for killing Jesus.

Jesus, God's Chosen Servant

¹⁵But Jesus knew what they were planning. He left that area, and many people followed him. He healed all the sick among them, ¹⁶but he warned them not to say who he was. ¹⁷This fulfilled the prophecy of Isaiah concerning him:
¹⁸"Look at my Servant,
     whom I have chosen.
   He is my Beloved,
     and I am very pleased with him.
   I will put my Spirit upon him,
     and he will proclaim justice to the nations.
¹⁹He will not fight or shout;
     he will not raise his voice in public.

²⁰ He will not crush those who are weak,
  or quench the smallest hope,
  until he brings full justice with his final victory.
²¹ And his name will be the hope
  of all the world."*

Jesus and the Prince of Demons

²² Then a demon-possessed man, who was both blind and unable to talk, was brought to Jesus. He healed the man so that he could both speak and see. ²³ The crowd was amazed. "Could it be that Jesus is the Son of David, the Messiah?" they wondered out loud.

²⁴ But when the Pharisees heard about the miracle, they said, "No wonder he can cast out demons. He gets his power from Satan,* the prince of demons."

²⁵ Jesus knew their thoughts and replied, "Any kingdom at war with itself is doomed. A city or home divided against itself is doomed. ²⁶ And if Satan is casting out Satan, he is fighting against himself. His own kingdom will not survive. ²⁷ And if I am empowered by the prince of demons,* what about your own followers? They cast out demons, too, so they will judge you for what you have said. ²⁸ But if I am casting out demons by the Spirit of God, then the Kingdom of God has arrived among you. ²⁹ Let me illustrate this. You can't enter a strong man's house and rob him without first tying him up. Only then can his house be robbed!* ³⁰ Anyone who isn't helping me opposes me, and anyone who isn't working with me is actually working against me.

³¹ "Every sin or blasphemy can be forgiven—except blasphemy against the Holy Spirit, which can never be forgiven. ³² Anyone who blasphemes against me, the Son of Man, can be forgiven, but blasphemy against the Holy

Spirit will never be forgiven, either in this world or in the world to come.

33 "A tree is identified by its fruit. Make a tree good, and its fruit will be good. Make a tree bad, and its fruit will be bad. 34 You brood of snakes! How could evil men like you speak what is good and right? For whatever is in your heart determines what you say. 35 A good person produces good words from a good heart, and an evil person produces evil words from an evil heart. 36 And I tell you this, that you must give an account on judgement day of every idle word you speak. 37 The words you say now reflect your fate then; either you will be justified by them or you will be condemned."

The Sign of Jonah

38 One day some teachers of religious law and Pharisees came to Jesus and said, "Teacher, we want you to show us a miraculous sign to prove that you are from God."

39 But Jesus replied, "Only an evil, faithless generation would ask for a miraculous sign; but the only sign I will give them is the sign of the prophet Jonah. 40 For as Jonah was in the belly of the great fish for three days and three nights, so I, the Son of Man, will be in the heart of the earth for three days and three nights. 41 The people of Nineveh will rise up against this generation on judgement day and condemn it, because they repented at the preaching of Jonah. And now someone greater than Jonah is here—and you refuse to repent. 42 The queen of Sheba* will also rise up against this generation on judgement day and condemn it, because she came from a distant land to hear the wisdom of Solomon. And now

someone greater than Solomon is here—and you refuse to listen to him.

[43] "When an evil spirit leaves a person, it goes into the desert, seeking rest but finding none. [44] Then it says, 'I will return to the person I came from.' So it returns and finds its former home empty, swept, and clean. [45] Then the spirit finds seven other spirits more evil than itself, and they all enter the person and live there. And so that person is worse off than before. That will be the experience of this evil generation."

The True Family of Jesus

[46] As Jesus was speaking to the crowd, his mother and brothers were outside, wanting to talk with him. [47] Someone told Jesus, "Your mother and your brothers are outside, and they want to speak to you."

[48] Jesus asked, "Who is my mother? Who are my brothers?" [49] Then he pointed to his disciples and said, "These are my mother and brothers. [50] Anyone who does the will of my Father in heaven is my brother and sister and mother!"

CHAPTER 13

Story of the Farmer Scattering Seed

Later that same day, Jesus left the house and went down to the shore, [2] where an immense crowd soon gathered. He got into a boat, where he sat and taught as the people listened on the shore. [3] He told many stories such as this one:

"A farmer went out to plant some seed. [4] As he scattered it across his field, some seeds fell on a footpath, and the birds came and ate them. [5] Other seeds fell on shallow soil with underlying rock. The plants sprang up quickly, [6] but they soon wilted beneath the hot sun and died because the roots had no nourishment in the shallow soil. ⁷Other seeds fell among thorns that shot up and choked out the tender blades. ⁸But some seeds fell on fertile soil and produced a crop that was thirty, sixty, and even a hundred times as much as had been planted. ⁹Anyone who is willing to hear should listen and understand!"

¹⁰His disciples came and asked him, "Why do you always tell stories when you talk to the people?"

¹¹Then he explained to them, "You have been permitted to understand the secrets of the Kingdom of Heaven, but others have not. ¹²To those who are open to my teaching, more understanding will be given, and they will have an abundance of knowledge. But to those who are not listening, even what they have will be taken away from them. ¹³That is why I tell these stories, because people see what I do, but they don't really see. They hear what I say, but they don't really hear, and they don't understand. ¹⁴This fulfils the prophecy of Isaiah, which says:

'You will hear my words,
    but you will not understand;
you will see what I do,
    but you will not perceive its meaning.
¹⁵For the hearts of these people are hardened,
    and their ears cannot hear,
    and they have closed their eyes—
so their eyes cannot see,
    and their ears cannot hear,
    and their hearts cannot understand,
and they cannot turn to me
    and let me heal them.'*

[16] "But blessed are your eyes, because they see; and your ears, because they hear. [17] I assure you, many prophets and godly people have longed to see and hear what you have seen and heard, but they could not.

[18] "Now here is the explanation of the story I told about the farmer sowing grain: [19] The seed that fell on the hard path represents those who hear the Good News about the Kingdom and don't understand it. Then the evil one comes and snatches the seed away from their hearts. [20] The rocky soil represents those who hear the message and receive it with joy. [21] But like young plants in such soil, their roots don't go very deep. At first they get along fine, but they wilt as soon as they have problems or are persecuted because they believe the word. [22] The thorny ground represents those who hear and accept the Good News, but all too quickly the message is crowded out by the cares of this life and the lure of wealth, so no crop is produced. [23] The good soil represents the hearts of those who truly accept God's message and produce a huge harvest—thirty, sixty, or even a hundred times as much as had been planted."

Story of the Wheat and Weeds

[24] Here is another story Jesus told: "The Kingdom of Heaven is like a farmer who planted good seed in his field. [25] But that night as everyone slept, his enemy came and planted weeds among the wheat. [26] When the crop began to grow and produce grain, the weeds also grew. [27] The farmer's servants came and told him, 'Sir, the field where you planted that good seed is full of weeds!'

[28] "'An enemy has done it!' the farmer exclaimed.

"'Shall we pull out the weeds?' they asked.

[29] "He replied, 'No, you'll hurt the wheat if you do. [30] Let both grow together until the harvest. Then I will tell the harvesters to sort out the weeds and burn them and to put the wheat in the barn.'"

Illustration of the Mustard Seed

[31] Here is another illustration Jesus used: "The Kingdom of Heaven is like a mustard seed planted in a field. [32] It is the smallest of all seeds, but it becomes the largest of garden plants and grows into a tree where birds can come and find shelter in its branches."

Illustration of the Yeast

[33] Jesus also used this illustration: "The Kingdom of Heaven is like yeast used by a woman making bread. Even though she used a large amount* of flour, the yeast permeated every part of the dough."

[34] Jesus always used stories and illustrations like these when speaking to the crowds. In fact, he never spoke to them without using such parables. [35] This fulfilled the prophecy that said,

"I will speak to you in parables.
    I will explain mysteries hidden since the creation of the world."*

The Wheat and Weeds Explained

[36] Then, leaving the crowds outside, Jesus went into the house. His disciples said, "Please explain the story of the weeds in the field."

[37] "All right," he said. "I, the Son of Man, am the farmer who plants the good seed. [38] The field is the world, and the good seed represents the people of the Kingdom. The

weeds are the people who belong to the evil one. ³⁹ The enemy who planted the weeds among the wheat is the Devil. The harvest is the end of the world, and the harvesters are the angels.

⁴⁰ "Just as the weeds are separated out and burned, so it will be at the end of the world. ⁴¹ I, the Son of Man, will send my angels, and they will remove from my Kingdom everything that causes sin and all who do evil, ⁴² and they will throw them into the furnace and burn them. There will be weeping and gnashing of teeth. ⁴³ Then the godly will shine like the sun in their Father's Kingdom. Anyone who is willing to hear should listen and understand!

Illustration of the Hidden Treasure

⁴⁴ "The Kingdom of Heaven is like a treasure that a man discovered hidden in a field. In his excitement, he hid it again and sold everything he owned to get enough money to buy the field—and to get the treasure, too!

Illustration of the Pearl Merchant

⁴⁵ "Again, the Kingdom of Heaven is like a pearl merchant on the lookout for choice pearls. ⁴⁶ When he discovered a pearl of great value, he sold everything he owned and bought it!

Illustration of the Fishing Net

⁴⁷ "Again, the Kingdom of Heaven is like a fishing net that is thrown into the water and gathers fish of every kind. ⁴⁸ When the net is full, they drag it up onto the shore, sit down, sort the good fish into crates, and throw the bad ones away. ⁴⁹ That is the way it will be at the end of the world. The angels will come and separate the wicked

people from the godly, ⁵⁰throwing the wicked into the fire. There will be weeping and gnashing of teeth. ⁵¹Do you understand?"

"Yes," they said, "we do."

⁵²Then he added, "Every teacher of religious law who has become a disciple in the Kingdom of Heaven is like a person who brings out of the storehouse the new teachings as well as the old."

Jesus Rejected at Nazareth

⁵³When Jesus had finished telling these stories, he left that part of the country. ⁵⁴He returned to Nazareth, his home town. When he taught there in the synagogue, everyone was astonished and said, "Where does he get his wisdom and his miracles? ⁵⁵He's just a carpenter's son, and we know Mary, his mother, and his brothers—James, Joseph, Simon, and Judas. ⁵⁶All his sisters live right here among us. What makes him so great?" ⁵⁷And they were deeply offended and refused to believe in him.

Then Jesus told them, "A prophet is honoured everywhere except in his own home town and among his own family." ⁵⁸And so he did only a few miracles there because of their unbelief.

CHAPTER 14

The Death of John the Baptist

When Herod Antipas* heard about Jesus, ²he said to his advisers, "This must be John the Baptist come back to life again! That is why he can do such miracles." ³For Herod had arrested and imprisoned John as a favour to his wife Herodias (the former wife of Herod's brother Philip). ⁴John kept telling Herod, "It is illegal for you to marry her." [5] Herod would have executed John, but he was afraid of a riot, because all the people believed John was a prophet.

[6] But at a birthday party for Herod, Herodias's daughter performed a dance that greatly pleased him, [7] so he promised with an oath to give her anything she wanted. [8] At her mother's urging, the girl asked, "I want the head of John the Baptist on a tray!" [9] The king was sorry, but because of his oath and because he didn't want to back down in front of his guests, he issued the necessary orders. [10] So John was beheaded in the prison, [11] and his head was brought on a tray and given to the girl, who took it to her mother. [12] John's disciples came for his body and buried it. Then they told Jesus what had happened.

Jesus Feeds Five Thousand

[13] As soon as Jesus heard the news, he went off by himself in a boat to a remote area to be alone. But the crowds heard where he was heading and followed by land from many villages. [14] A vast crowd was there as he stepped from the boat, and he had compassion on them and healed their sick.

[15] That evening the disciples came to him and said, "This is a desolate place, and it is getting late. Send the crowds away so they can go to the villages and buy food for themselves."

[16] But Jesus replied, "That isn't necessary—you feed them."

[17] "Impossible!" they exclaimed. "We have only five loaves of bread and two fish!"

[18] "Bring them here," he said. [19] Then he told the people to sit down on the grass. And he took the five loaves and two fish, looked up towards heaven, and asked God's blessing on the food. Breaking the loaves into pieces, he gave some of the bread and fish to each disciple, and the disciples

gave them to the people. ²⁰ They all ate as much as they wanted, and they picked up twelve baskets of leftovers. ²¹ About five thousand men had eaten from those five loaves, in addition to all the women and children!

Jesus Walks on Water

²² Immediately after this, Jesus made his disciples get back into the boat and cross to the other side of the lake while he sent the people home. ²³ Afterwards he went up into the hills by himself to pray. Night fell while he was there alone. ²⁴ Meanwhile, the disciples were in trouble far away from land, for a strong wind had risen, and they were fighting heavy waves.

²⁵ About three o'clock in the morning* Jesus came to them, walking on the water. ²⁶ When the disciples saw him, they screamed in terror, thinking he was a ghost. ²⁷ But Jesus spoke to them at once. "It's all right," he said. "I am here! Don't be afraid."

²⁸ Then Peter called to him, "Lord, if it's really you, tell me to come to you by walking on the water."

²⁹ "All right, come," Jesus said.

So Peter went over the side of the boat and walked on the water towards Jesus. ³⁰ But when he looked around at the high waves, he was terrified and began to sink. "Save me, Lord!" he shouted.

³¹ Instantly Jesus reached out his hand and grabbed him. "You don't have much faith," Jesus said. "Why did you doubt me?" ³² And when they climbed back into the boat, the wind stopped.

³³ Then the disciples worshipped him. "You really are the Son of God!" they exclaimed.

³⁴ After they had crossed the lake, they landed at Gennesaret. ³⁵ The news of their arrival spread quickly throughout the whole surrounding area, and soon people were bringing all their sick to be healed. ³⁶ The sick begged him to let them touch even the fringe of his robe, and all who touched it were healed.

CHAPTER 15

Jesus Teaches about Inner Purity

Some Pharisees and teachers of religious law now arrived from Jerusalem to interview Jesus. ² "Why do your disciples disobey our age-old traditions?" they demanded. "They ignore our tradition of ceremonial hand-washing before they eat."

³ Jesus replied, "And why do you, by your traditions, violate the direct commandments of God? ⁴ For instance, God says, 'Honour your father and mother,' and 'Anyone who speaks evil of father or mother must be put to death.'* ⁵ But you say, 'You don't need to honour your parents by caring for their needs if you give the money to God instead.' ⁶ And so, by your own tradition, you nullify the direct commandment of God. ⁷ You hypocrites! Isaiah was prophesying about you when he said,

⁸ 'These people honour me with their lips,
but their hearts are far away.
⁹ Their worship is a farce,
for they replace God's commands with their own
man-made teachings.'* "

¹⁰ Then Jesus called to the crowds and said, "Listen to what I say and try to understand. ¹¹ You are not defiled by what you eat; you are defiled by what you say and do.*"

[12] Then the disciples came to him and asked, "Do you realize you offended the Pharisees by what you just said?"

[13] Jesus replied, "Every plant not planted by my heavenly Father will be rooted up, [14] so ignore them. They are blind guides leading the blind, and if one blind person guides another, they will both fall into a ditch."

[15] Then Peter asked Jesus, "Explain what you meant when you said people aren't defiled by what they eat."

[16] "Don't you understand?" Jesus asked him. [17] "Anything you eat passes through the stomach and then goes out of the body. [18] But evil words come from an evil heart and defile the person who says them. [19] For from the heart come evil thoughts, murder, adultery, all other sexual immorality, theft, lying, and slander. [20] These are what defile you. Eating with unwashed hands could never defile you and make you unacceptable to God!"

The Faith of a Gentile Woman

[21] Jesus then left Galilee and went north to the region of Tyre and Sidon. [22] A Gentile* woman who lived there came to him, pleading, "Have mercy on me, O Lord, Son of David! For my daughter has a demon in her, and it is severely tormenting her."

[23] But Jesus gave her no reply—not even a word. Then his disciples urged him to send her away. "Tell her to leave," they said. "She is bothering us with all her begging."

[24] Then he said to the woman, "I was sent only to help the people of Israel—God's lost sheep—not the Gentiles."

[25] But she came and worshipped him and pleaded again, "Lord, help me!"

[26] "It isn't right to take food from the children and throw it to the dogs," he said.

[27] "Yes, Lord," she replied, "but even dogs are permitted to eat crumbs that fall beneath their master's table."

[28] "Woman," Jesus said to her, "your faith is great. Your request is granted." And her daughter was instantly healed.

Jesus Heals Many People

[29] Jesus returned to the Sea of Galilee and climbed a hill and sat down. [30] A vast crowd brought him the lame, blind, crippled, mute, and many others with physical difficulties, and they laid them before Jesus. And he healed them all. [31] The crowd was amazed! Those who hadn't been able to speak were talking, the crippled were made well, the lame were walking around, and those who had been blind could see again! And they praised the God of Israel.

Jesus Feeds Four Thousand

[32] Then Jesus called his disciples to him and said, "I feel sorry for these people. They have been here with me for three days, and they have nothing left to eat. I don't want to send them away hungry, or they will faint along the road."

[33] The disciples replied, "And where would we get enough food out here in the wilderness for all of them to eat?"

[34] Jesus asked, "How many loaves of bread do you have?"

They replied, "Seven, and a few small fish." [35] So Jesus told all the people to sit down on the ground. [36] Then he took the seven loaves and the fish, thanked God for them, broke them into pieces, and gave them to the disciples, who distributed the food to the crowd.

[37] They all ate until they were full, and when the scraps were picked up, there were seven large baskets of food left over! [38] There were four thousand men who were fed that day, in addition to all the women and children. [39] Then

Jesus sent the people home, and he got into a boat and crossed over to the region of Magadan.

CHAPTER 16

Leaders Demand a Miraculous Sign

One day the Pharisees and Sadducees came to test Jesus' claims by asking him to show them a miraculous sign from heaven.

²He replied, "You know the saying, 'Red sky at night means fair weather tomorrow, ³red sky in the morning means foul weather all day.' You are good at reading the weather signs in the sky, but you can't read the obvious signs of the times!* ⁴Only an evil, faithless generation would ask for a miraculous sign, but the only sign I will give them is the sign of the prophet Jonah." Then Jesus left them and went away.

Yeast of the Pharisees and Sadducees

⁵Later, after they crossed to the other side of the lake, the disciples discovered they had forgotten to bring any food. ⁶"Watch out!" Jesus warned them. "Beware of the yeast of the Pharisees and Sadducees."

⁷They decided he was saying this because they hadn't brought any bread. ⁸Jesus knew what they were thinking, so he said, "You have so little faith! Why are you worried about having no food? ⁹Won't you ever understand? Don't you remember the five thousand I fed with five loaves, and the baskets of food that were left over? ¹⁰Don't you remember the four thousand I fed with seven loaves, with baskets of food left over? ¹¹How could you even think I was talking about food? So again I say, 'Beware of the yeast of the Pharisees and Sadducees.'"

¹²Then at last they understood that he wasn't speaking about yeast or bread but about the false teaching of the Pharisees and Sadducees.

Peter's Declaration about Jesus

¹³When Jesus came to the region of Caesarea Philippi, he asked his disciples, "Who do people say that the Son of Man is?"

¹⁴"Well," they replied, "some say John the Baptist, some say Elijah, and others say Jeremiah or one of the other prophets."

¹⁵Then he asked them, "Who do you say I am?"

¹⁶Simon Peter answered, "You are the Messiah, the Son of the living God."

¹⁷Jesus replied, "You are blessed, Simon son of John,* because my Father in heaven has revealed this to you. You did not learn this from any human being. ¹⁸Now I say to you that you are Peter,*ᵃ and upon this rock I will build my church, and all the powers of hell*ᵇ will not conquer it. ¹⁹And I will give you the keys of the Kingdom of Heaven. Whatever you lock on earth will be locked in heaven, and whatever you open on earth will be opened in heaven." ²⁰Then he sternly warned them not to tell anyone that he was the Messiah.

Jesus Predicts His Death

²¹From then on Jesus began to tell his disciples plainly that he had to go to Jerusalem, and he told them what would happen to him there. He would suffer at the hands of the leaders and the leading priests and the teachers of religious law. He would be killed, and he would be raised on the third day.

²²But Peter took him aside and began to reprimand him. "Heaven forbid, Lord," he said. "This will never happen to you!"

²³Jesus turned to Peter and said, "Get away from me, Satan! You are a dangerous trap to me. You are seeing things merely from a human point of view, and not from God's."

²⁴Then Jesus said to the disciples, "If any of you wants to be my follower, you must put aside your selfish ambition, shoulder your cross, and follow me. ²⁵If you try to keep your life for yourself, you will lose it. But if you give up your life for me, you will find true life. ²⁶And how do you benefit if you gain the whole world but lose your own soul* in the process? Is anything worth more than your soul? ²⁷For I, the Son of Man, will come in the glory of my Father with his angels and will judge all people according to their deeds. ²⁸And I assure you that some of you standing here right now will not die before you see me, the Son of Man, coming in my Kingdom."

CHAPTER 17

The Transfiguration

Six days later Jesus took Peter and the two brothers, James and John, and led them up a high mountain. ²As the men watched, Jesus' appearance changed so that his face shone like the sun, and his clothing became dazzling white. ³Suddenly, Moses and Elijah appeared and began talking with Jesus. ⁴Peter blurted out, "Lord, this is wonderful! If you want me to, I'll make three shrines,* one for you, one for Moses, and one for Elijah."

⁵But even as he said it, a bright cloud came over them, and a voice from the cloud said, "This is my beloved Son, and I am fully pleased with him. Listen to him." ⁶The disciples were terrified and fell face down on the ground.

⁷Jesus came over and touched them. "Get up," he said, "don't be afraid." ⁸And when they looked, they saw only Jesus with them. ⁹As they descended the mountain, Jesus commanded them, "Don't tell anyone what you have seen until I, the Son of Man, have been raised from the dead."

¹⁰His disciples asked, "Why do the teachers of religious law insist that Elijah must return before the Messiah comes*?"

¹¹Jesus replied, "Elijah is indeed coming first to set everything in order. ¹²But I tell you, he has already come, but he wasn't recognized, and he was badly mistreated. And soon the Son of Man will also suffer at their hands." ¹³Then the disciples realized he had been speaking of John the Baptist.

Jesus Heals a Demon-Possessed Boy

¹⁴When they arrived at the foot of the mountain, a huge crowd was waiting for them. A man came and knelt before Jesus and said, ¹⁵"Lord, have mercy on my son, because he has seizures and suffers terribly. He often falls into the fire or into the water. ¹⁶So I brought him to your disciples, but they couldn't heal him."

¹⁷Jesus replied, "You stubborn, faithless people! How long must I be with you until you believe? How long must I put up with you? Bring the boy to me." ¹⁸Then Jesus rebuked the demon in the boy, and it left him. From that moment the boy was well.

¹⁹Afterwards the disciples asked Jesus privately, "Why couldn't we cast out that demon?"

[20]"You didn't have enough faith," Jesus told them. "I assure you, even if you had faith as small as a mustard seed you could say to this mountain, 'Move from here to there,' and it would move. Nothing would be impossible."*

Jesus Again Predicts His Death

[22]One day after they had returned to Galilee, Jesus told them, "The Son of Man is going to be betrayed. [23]He will be killed, but three days later he will be raised from the dead." And the disciples' hearts were filled with grief.

Payment of the Temple Tax

[24]On their arrival in Capernaum, the tax collectors for the Temple tax came to Peter and asked him, "Doesn't your teacher pay the Temple tax?"

[25]"Of course he does," Peter replied. Then he went into the house to talk to Jesus about it.

But before he had a chance to speak, Jesus asked him, "What do you think, Peter*? Do kings tax their own people or the foreigners they have conquered?"

[26]"They tax the foreigners," Peter replied.

"Well, then," Jesus said, "the citizens are free! [27]However, we don't want to offend them, so go down to the lake and throw in a line. Open the mouth of the first fish you catch, and you will find a coin. Take the coin and pay the tax for both of us."

CHAPTER 18

The Greatest in the Kingdom

About that time the disciples came to Jesus and asked, "Which of us is greatest in the Kingdom of Heaven?"

² Jesus called a small child over to him and put the child among them. ³ Then he said, "I assure you, unless you turn from your sins and become as little children, you will never get into the Kingdom of Heaven. ⁴ Therefore, anyone who becomes as humble as this little child is the greatest in the Kingdom of Heaven. ⁵ And anyone who welcomes a little child like this on my behalf is welcoming me. ⁶ But if anyone causes one of these little ones who trusts in me to lose faith, it would be better for that person to be thrown into the sea with a large millstone tied around the neck.

⁷ "How terrible it will be for anyone who causes others to sin. Temptation to do wrong is inevitable, but how terrible it will be for the person who does the tempting. ⁸ So if your hand or foot causes you to sin, cut it off and throw it away. It is better to enter heaven* crippled or lame than to be thrown into the unquenchable fire with both of your hands and feet. ⁹ And if your eye causes you to sin, gouge it out and throw it away. It is better to enter heaven half blind than to have two eyes and be thrown into hell.

¹⁰ "Beware that you don't despise a single one of these little ones. For I tell you that in heaven their angels are always in the presence of my heavenly Father.*

Story of the Lost Sheep

¹² "If a shepherd has a hundred sheep, and one wanders away and is lost, what will he do? Won't he leave the ninety-nine others and go out into the hills to search for the

lost one? ¹³ And if he finds it, he will surely rejoice over it more than over the ninety-nine that didn't wander away! ¹⁴ In the same way, it is not my heavenly Father's will that even one of these little ones should perish.

Correcting a Fellow Believer

¹⁵ "If another believer* sins against you, go privately and point out the fault. If the other person listens and confesses it, you have won that person back. ¹⁶ But if you are unsuccessful, take one or two others with you and go back again, so that everything you say may be confirmed by two or three witnesses. ¹⁷ If that person still refuses to listen, take your case to the church. If the church decides you are right, but the other person won't accept it, treat that person as a pagan or a corrupt tax collector. ¹⁸ I tell you this: Whatever you prohibit on earth is prohibited in heaven, and whatever you allow on earth is allowed in heaven.

¹⁹ "I also tell you this: If two of you agree here on earth concerning anything you ask, my Father in heaven will do it for you. ²⁰ For where two or three gather together because they are mine,* I am there among them."

Story of the Unforgiving Debtor

²¹ Then Peter came to him and asked, "Lord, how often should I forgive someone* who sins against me? Seven times?"

²² "No!" Jesus replied, "seventy times seven!*

²³ "For this reason, the Kingdom of Heaven can be compared to a king who decided to bring his accounts up to date with servants who had borrowed money from him. ²⁴ In the process, one of his debtors was brought in who owed him millions of pounds.* ²⁵ He couldn't pay, so the

king ordered that he, his wife, his children, and everything he had be sold to pay the debt. ²⁶But the man fell down before the king and begged him, 'Oh, sir, be patient with me, and I will pay it all.' ²⁷Then the king was filled with pity for him, and he released him and forgave his debt.

²⁸"But when the man left the king, he went to a fellow servant who owed him a few thousand pounds.* He grabbed him by the throat and demanded instant payment. ²⁹His fellow servant fell down before him and begged for a little more time. 'Be patient and I will pay it,' he pleaded. ³⁰But his creditor wouldn't wait. He had the man arrested and jailed until the debt could be paid in full.

³¹"When some of the other servants saw this, they were very upset. They went to the king and told him what had happened. ³²Then the king called in the man he had forgiven and said, 'You evil servant! I forgave you that tremendous debt because you pleaded with me. ³³Shouldn't you have mercy on your fellow servant, just as I had mercy on you?' ³⁴Then the angry king sent the man to prison until he had paid every penny.

³⁵"That's what my heavenly Father will do to you if you refuse to forgive your brothers and sisters* in your heart."

CHAPTER 19

Discussion about Divorce and Marriage

After Jesus had finished saying these things, he left Galilee and went southward to the region of Judea and into the area east of the River Jordan. ²Vast crowds followed him there, and he healed their sick.

³ Some Pharisees came and tried to trap him with this question: "Should a man be allowed to divorce his wife for any reason?"

⁴ "Haven't you read the Scriptures?" Jesus replied. "They record that from the beginning 'God made them male and female.'* ⁵ And he said, 'This explains why a man leaves his father and mother and is joined to his wife, and the two are united into one.'* ⁶ Since they are no longer two but one, let no one separate them, for God has joined them together."

⁷ "Then why did Moses say a man could merely write an official letter of divorce and send her away?"* they asked.

⁸ Jesus replied, "Moses permitted divorce as a concession to your hard-hearted wickedness, but it was not what God had originally intended. ⁹ And I tell you this, a man who divorces his wife and marries another commits adultery—unless his wife has been unfaithful.*"

¹⁰ Jesus' disciples then said to him, "Then it is better not to marry!"

¹¹ "Not everyone can accept this statement," Jesus said. "Only those whom God helps. ¹² Some are born as eunuchs, some have been made that way by others, and some choose not to marry for the sake of the Kingdom of Heaven. Let anyone who can, accept this statement."

Jesus Blesses the Children

¹³ Some children were brought to Jesus so he could lay his hands on them and pray for them. The disciples told them not to bother him. ¹⁴ But Jesus said, "Let the children come to me. Don't stop them! For the Kingdom of Heaven belongs to such as these." ¹⁵ And he put his hands on their heads and blessed them before he left.

The Rich Young Man

[16] Someone came to Jesus with this question: "Teacher,* what good things must I do to have eternal life?"

[17] "Why ask me about what is good?" Jesus replied. "Only God is good. But to answer your question, you can receive eternal life if you keep the commandments."

[18] "Which ones?" the man asked.

And Jesus replied: " 'Do not murder. Do not commit adultery. Do not steal. Do not testify falsely. [19] Honour your father and mother. Love your neighbour as yourself.'* "

[20] "I've obeyed all these commandments," the young man replied. "What else must I do?"

[21] Jesus told him, "If you want to be perfect, go and sell all you have and give the money to the poor, and you will have treasure in heaven. Then come, follow me." [22] But when the young man heard this, he went away sadly because he had many possessions.

[23] Then Jesus said to his disciples, "I tell you the truth, it is very hard for a rich person to get into the Kingdom of Heaven. [24] I say it again—it is easier for a camel to go through the eye of a needle than for a rich person to enter the Kingdom of God!"

[25] The disciples were astounded. "Then who in the world can be saved?" they asked.

[26] Jesus looked at them intently and said, "Humanly speaking, it is impossible. But with God everything is possible."

[27] Then Peter said to him, "We've given up everything to follow you. What will we get out of it?"

[28] And Jesus replied, "I assure you that when I, the Son of Man, sit upon my glorious throne in the Kingdom,* you who have been my followers will also sit on twelve thrones,

judging the twelve tribes of Israel. ²⁹And everyone who has given up houses or brothers or sisters or father or mother or children or property, for my sake, will receive a hundred times as much in return and will have eternal life. ³⁰But many who seem to be important now will be the least important then, and those who are considered least here will be the greatest then.*

CHAPTER 20

Story of the Vineyard Workers

"For the Kingdom of Heaven is like the owner of an estate who went out early one morning to hire workers for his vineyard. ²He agreed to pay the normal daily wage* and sent them out to work.

³"At nine o'clock in the morning he was passing through the marketplace and saw some people standing around doing nothing. ⁴So he hired them, telling them he would pay them whatever was right at the end of the day. ⁵At noon and again around three o'clock he did the same thing. ⁶At five o'clock that evening he was in town again and saw some more people standing around. He asked them, 'Why haven't you been working today?'

⁷"They replied, 'Because no one hired us.'

"The owner of the estate told them, 'Then go on out and join the others in my vineyard.'

⁸"That evening he told the foreman to call the workers in and pay them, beginning with the last workers first. ⁹When those hired at five o'clock were paid, each received a full day's wage. ¹⁰When those hired earlier came to get their pay, they assumed they would receive more. But they, too, were paid a day's wage. ¹¹When they received their pay,

they protested, ¹²'Those people worked only one hour, and yet you've paid them just as much as you paid us who worked all day in the scorching heat.'

¹³ "He answered one of them, 'Friend, I haven't been unfair! Didn't you agree to work all day for the usual wage? ¹⁴Take it and go. I wanted to pay this last worker the same as you. ¹⁵Is it against the law for me to do what I want with my money? Should you be angry because I am kind?'

¹⁶ "And so it is, that many who are first now will be last then; and those who are last now will be first then."

Jesus Again Predicts His Death

¹⁷As Jesus was on the way to Jerusalem, he took the twelve disciples aside privately and told them what was going to happen to him. ¹⁸"When we get to Jerusalem," he said, "the Son of Man will be betrayed to the leading priests and the teachers of religious law. They will sentence him to die. ¹⁹Then they will hand him over to the Romans to be mocked, whipped, and crucified. But on the third day he will be raised from the dead."

Jesus Teaches about Serving Others

²⁰Then the mother of James and John, the sons of Zebedee, came to Jesus with her sons. She knelt respectfully to ask a favour. ²¹"What is your request?" he asked.

She replied, "In your Kingdom, will you let my two sons sit in places of honour next to you, one at your right and the other at your left?"

²²But Jesus told them, "You don't know what you are asking! Are you able to drink from the bitter cup of sorrow I am about to drink?"

"Oh yes," they replied, "we are able!"

²³"You will indeed drink from it," he told them. "But I have no right to say who will sit on the thrones next to mine. My Father has prepared those places for the ones he has chosen."

²⁴When the ten other disciples heard what James and John had asked, they were indignant. ²⁵But Jesus called them together and said, "You know that in this world kings are tyrants, and officials lord it over the people beneath them. ²⁶But among you it should be quite different. Whoever wants to be a leader among you must be your servant, ²⁷and whoever wants to be first must become your slave. ²⁸For even I, the Son of Man, came here not to be served but to serve others, and to give my life as a ransom for many."

Jesus Heals Two Blind Men

²⁹As Jesus and the disciples left the city of Jericho, a huge crowd followed behind. ³⁰Two blind men were sitting beside the road. When they heard that Jesus was coming that way, they began shouting, "Lord, Son of David, have mercy on us!" ³¹The crowd told them to be quiet, but they only shouted louder, "Lord, Son of David, have mercy on us!"

³²Jesus stopped in the road and called, "What do you want me to do for you?"

³³"Lord," they said, "we want to see!" ³⁴Jesus felt sorry for them and touched their eyes. Instantly they could see! Then they followed him.

CHAPTER 21

The Triumphal Entry

As Jesus and the disciples approached Jerusalem, they came to the town of Bethphage on the Mount of Olives. Jesus sent two of them on ahead. ²"Go into the village over there," he said, "and you will see a donkey tied there, with its colt beside it. Untie them and bring them here. ³If anyone asks what you are doing, just say, 'The Lord needs them,' and he will immediately send them." ⁴This was done to fulfil the prophecy,
⁵ "Tell the people of Israel,*ᵃ

'Look, your King is coming to you.
He is humble, riding on a donkey—
even on a donkey's colt.' "*ᵇ
⁶The two disciples did as Jesus said. ⁷They brought the animals to him and threw their garments over the colt, and he sat on it.*

⁸Most of the crowd spread their coats on the road ahead of Jesus, and others cut branches from the trees and spread them on the road. ⁹He was in the centre of the procession, and the crowds all around him were shouting,

"Praise God*ᵃ for the Son of David!
Bless the one who comes in the name of the Lord!
Praise God in highest heaven!"*ᵇ
¹⁰The entire city of Jerusalem was stirred as he entered. "Who is this?" they asked.
¹¹And the crowds replied, "It's Jesus, the prophet from Nazareth in Galilee."

Jesus Clears the Temple

[12] Jesus entered the Temple and began to drive out the merchants and their customers. He knocked over the tables of the money changers and the stalls of those selling doves. [13] He said, "The Scriptures declare, 'My Temple will be called a place of prayer,' but you have turned it into a den of thieves!"*

[14] The blind and the lame came to him, and he healed them there in the Temple. [15] The leading priests and the teachers of religious law saw these wonderful miracles and heard even the little children in the Temple shouting, "Praise God for the Son of David." But they were indignant [16] and asked Jesus, "Do you hear what these children are saying?"

"Yes," Jesus replied. "Haven't you ever read the Scriptures? For they say, 'You have taught children and infants to give you praise.'*" [17] Then he returned to Bethany, where he stayed overnight.

Jesus Curses the Fig Tree

[18] In the morning, as Jesus was returning to Jerusalem, he was hungry, [19] and he noticed a fig tree beside the road. He went over to see if there were any figs on it, but there were only leaves. Then he said to it, "May you never bear fruit again!" And immediately the fig tree withered up.

[20] The disciples were amazed when they saw this and asked, "How did the fig tree wither so quickly?"

[21] Then Jesus told them, "I assure you, if you have faith and don't doubt, you can do things like this and much more. You can even say to this mountain, 'May God lift you up and throw you into the sea,' and it will happen. [22] If you believe, you will receive whatever you ask for in prayer."

The Authority of Jesus Challenged

²³ When Jesus returned to the Temple and began teaching, the leading priests and other leaders came up to him. They demanded, "By whose authority did you drive out the merchants from the Temple?* Who gave you such authority?"

²⁴ "I'll tell you who gave me the authority to do these things if you answer one question," Jesus replied. ²⁵ "Did John's baptism come from heaven or was it merely human?"

They talked it over among themselves. "If we say it was from heaven, he will ask why we didn't believe him. ²⁶ But if we say it was merely human, we'll be mobbed, because the people think he was a prophet." ²⁷ So they finally replied, "We don't know."

And Jesus responded, "Then I won't answer your question either.

Story of the Two Sons

²⁸ "But what do you think about this? A man with two sons told the older boy, 'Son, go out and work in the vineyard today.' ²⁹ The son answered, 'No, I won't go,' but later he changed his mind and went anyway. ³⁰ Then the father told the other son, 'You go,' and he said, 'Yes, sir, I will.' But he didn't go. ³¹ Which of the two was obeying his father?"

They replied, "The first, of course."

Then Jesus explained his meaning: "I assure you, corrupt tax collectors and prostitutes will get into the Kingdom of God before you do. ³² For John the Baptist came and showed you the way to life, and you didn't believe him, while tax collectors and prostitutes did. And even when you saw this happening, you refused to turn from your sins and believe him.

Story of the Evil Farmers

[33] "Now listen to this story. A certain landowner planted a vineyard, built a wall around it, dug a pit for pressing out the grape juice, and built a lookout tower. Then he leased the vineyard to tenant farmers and moved to another country. [34] At the time of the grape harvest he sent his servants to collect his share of the crop. [35] But the farmers grabbed his servants, beat one, killed one, and stoned another. [36] So the landowner sent a larger group of his servants to collect for him, but the results were the same.

[37] "Finally, the owner sent his son, thinking, 'Surely they will respect my son.'

[38] "But when the farmers saw his son coming, they said to one another, 'Here comes the heir to this estate. Come on, let's kill him and get the estate for ourselves!' [39] So they grabbed him, took him out of the vineyard, and murdered him.

[40] "When the owner of the vineyard returns," Jesus asked, "what do you think he will do to those farmers?"

[41] The religious leaders replied, "He will put the wicked men to a horrible death and lease the vineyard to others who will give him his share of the crop after each harvest."

[42] Then Jesus asked them, "Didn't you ever read this in the Scriptures?

'The stone rejected by the builders
   has now become the cornerstone.
This is the Lord's doing,
   and it is marvellous to see.'*

[43] What I mean is that the Kingdom of God will be taken away from you and given to a nation that will produce the proper fruit. [44] Anyone who stumbles over that stone will be broken to pieces, and it will crush anyone on whom it falls.'"

⁴⁵When the leading priests and Pharisees heard Jesus, they realized he was pointing at them—that they were the farmers in his story. ⁴⁶They wanted to arrest him, but they were afraid to try because the crowds considered Jesus to be a prophet.

CHAPTER 22

Story of the Great Feast

Jesus told them several other stories to illustrate the Kingdom. He said, ²"The Kingdom of Heaven can be illustrated by the story of a king who prepared a great wedding feast for his son. ³Many guests were invited, and when the banquet was ready, he sent his servants to notify everyone that it was time to come. But they all refused! ⁴So he sent other servants to tell them, 'The feast has been prepared, and choice meats have been cooked. Everything is ready. Hurry!' ⁵But the guests he had invited ignored them and went about their business, one to his farm, another to his store. ⁶Others seized his messengers and treated them shamefully, even killing some of them.

⁷"Then the king became furious. He sent out his army to destroy the murderers and burn their city. ⁸And he said to his servants, 'The wedding feast is ready, and the guests I invited aren't worthy of the honour. ⁹Now go out to the street corners and invite everyone you see.'

¹⁰"So the servants brought in everyone they could find, good and bad alike, and the banquet hall was filled with guests. ¹¹But when the king came in to meet the guests, he noticed a man who wasn't wearing the proper clothes for a wedding. ¹²'Friend,' he asked, 'how is it that you are here without wedding clothes?' And the man had no reply.

¹³ Then the king said to his aides, 'Bind him hand and foot and throw him out into the outer darkness, where there is weeping and gnashing of teeth.' ¹⁴ For many are called, but few are chosen."

Taxes for Caesar

¹⁵ Then the Pharisees met together to think of a way to trap Jesus into saying something for which they could accuse him. ¹⁶ They decided to send some of their disciples, along with the supporters of Herod, to ask him this question: "Teacher, we know how honest you are. You teach about the way of God regardless of the consequences. You are impartial and don't have favourites. ¹⁷ Now tell us what you think about this: Is it right to pay taxes to the Roman government or not?"

¹⁸ But Jesus knew their evil motives. "You hypocrites!" he said. "Whom are you trying to fool with your trick questions? ¹⁹ Here, show me the Roman coin used for the tax." When they handed him the coin,* ²⁰ he asked, "Whose picture and title are stamped on it?"

²¹ "Caesar's," they replied.

"Well, then," he said, "give to Caesar what belongs to him. But everything that belongs to God must be given to God." ²² His reply amazed them, and they went away.

Discussion about Resurrection

²³ That same day Jesus was approached by some Sadducees—a group of Jews who say there is no resurrection after death. They posed this question: ²⁴ "Teacher, Moses said, 'If a man dies without children, his brother should marry the widow and have a child who will be the brother's heir.'* ²⁵ Well, there were seven brothers. The oldest

married and then died without children, so the second brother married the widow. ²⁶This brother also died without children, and the wife was married to the next brother, and so on until she had been the wife of each of them. ²⁷And then she also died. ²⁸So tell us, whose wife will she be in the resurrection? For she was the wife of all seven of them!"

²⁹Jesus replied, "Your problem is that you don't know the Scriptures, and you don't know the power of God. ³⁰For when the dead rise, they won't be married. They will be like the angels in heaven. ³¹But now, as to whether there will be a resurrection of the dead—haven't you ever read about this in the Scriptures? Long after Abraham, Isaac, and Jacob had died, God said,* ³²'I am the God of Abraham, the God of Isaac, and the God of Jacob.'* So he is the God of the living, not the dead."

³³When the crowds heard him, they were impressed with his teaching.

The Most Important Commandment

³⁴But when the Pharisees heard that he had silenced the Sadducees with his reply, they thought up a fresh question of their own to ask him. ³⁵One of them, an expert in religious law, tried to trap him with this question: ³⁶"Teacher, which is the most important commandment in the law of Moses?"

³⁷Jesus replied, " 'You must love the Lord your God with all your heart, all your soul, and all your mind.'* ³⁸This is the first and greatest commandment. ³⁹A second is equally important: 'Love your neighbour as yourself.'* ⁴⁰All the other commandments and all the demands of the prophets are based on these two commandments."

Whose Son Is the Messiah?

⁴¹ Then, surrounded by the Pharisees, Jesus asked them a question: ⁴² "What do you think about the Messiah? Whose son is he?"

They replied, "He is the son of David."

⁴³ Jesus responded, "Then why does David, speaking under the inspiration of the Holy Spirit, call him Lord? For David said,

⁴⁴ 'The LORD said to my Lord,
  Sit in honour at my right hand
    until I humble your enemies beneath your feet.'*

⁴⁵ Since David called him Lord, how can he be his son at the same time?"

⁴⁶ No one could answer him. And after that, no one dared to ask him any more questions.

CHAPTER 23

Jesus Warns the Religious Leaders

Then Jesus said to the crowds and to his disciples, ² "The teachers of religious law and the Pharisees are the official interpreters of the Scriptures. ³ So practise and obey whatever they say to you, but don't follow their example. For they don't practise what they teach. ⁴ They crush you with impossible religious demands and never lift a finger to help ease the burden.

⁵ "Everything they do is for show. On their arms they wear extra wide prayer boxes with Scripture verses inside,* and they wear extra long tassels on their robes. ⁶ And how they love to sit at the head table at banquets and in the most prominent seats in the synagogue! ⁷ They enjoy the attention

they get on the streets, and they enjoy being called 'Rabbi.'*
⁸Don't ever let anyone call you 'Rabbi,' for you have only one teacher, and all of you are on the same level as brothers and sisters.* ⁹And don't address anyone here on earth as 'Father,' for only God in heaven is your spiritual Father. ¹⁰And don't let anyone call you 'Master,' for there is only one master, the Messiah. ¹¹The greatest among you must be a servant. ¹²But those who exalt themselves will be humbled, and those who humble themselves will be exalted.

¹³"How terrible it will be for you teachers of religious law and you Pharisees. Hypocrites! For you won't let others enter the Kingdom of Heaven, and you won't go in yourselves.* ¹⁵Yes, how terrible it will be for you teachers of religious law and you Pharisees. For you cross land and sea to make one convert, and then you turn him into twice the son of hell as you yourselves are.

¹⁶"Blind guides! How terrible it will be for you! For you say that it means nothing to swear 'by God's Temple'—you can break that oath. But then you say that it is binding to swear 'by the gold in the Temple.' ¹⁷Blind fools! Which is greater, the gold, or the Temple that makes the gold sacred? ¹⁸And you say that to take an oath 'by the altar' can be broken, but to swear 'by the gifts on the altar' is binding! ¹⁹How blind! For which is greater, the gift on the altar, or the altar that makes the gift sacred? ²⁰When you swear 'by the altar,' you are swearing by it and by everything on it. ²¹And when you swear 'by the Temple,' you are swearing by it and by God, who lives in it. ²²And when you swear 'by heaven,' you are swearing by the throne of God and by God, who sits on the throne.

²³"How terrible it will be for you teachers of religious law and you Pharisees. Hypocrites! For you are careful to tithe

even the tiniest part of your income,* but you ignore the important things of the law—justice, mercy, and faith. You should tithe, yes, but you should not leave undone the more important things. ²⁴Blind guides! You strain your water so you won't accidentally swallow a gnat; then you swallow a camel!

²⁵ "How terrible it will be for you teachers of religious law and you Pharisees. Hypocrites! You are so careful to clean the outside of the cup and the dish, but inside you are filthy—full of greed and self-indulgence! ²⁶Blind Pharisees! First wash the inside of the cup, and then the outside will become clean, too.

²⁷ "How terrible it will be for you teachers of religious law and you Pharisees. Hypocrites! You are like whitewashed tombs—beautiful on the outside but filled on the inside with dead people's bones and all sorts of impurity. ²⁸You try to look like upright people outwardly, but inside your hearts are filled with hypocrisy and lawlessness.

²⁹ "How terrible it will be for you teachers of religious law and you Pharisees. Hypocrites! For you build tombs for the prophets your ancestors killed and decorate the graves of the godly people your ancestors destroyed. ³⁰Then you say, 'We never would have joined them in killing the prophets.'

³¹ "In saying that, you are accusing yourselves of being the descendants of those who murdered the prophets. ³²Go ahead. Finish what they started. ³³Snakes! Sons of vipers! How will you escape the judgement of hell? ³⁴I will send you prophets and wise men and teachers of religious law. You will kill some by crucifixion and whip others in your synagogues, chasing them from city to city. ³⁵As a result, you will become guilty of murdering all the godly people from righteous Abel to Zechariah son of Barachiah, whom

you murdered in the Temple between the altar and the sanctuary. ³⁶I assure you, all the accumulated judgement of the centuries will break upon the heads of this very generation.

Jesus Grieves over Jerusalem

³⁷"O Jerusalem, Jerusalem, the city that kills the prophets and stones God's messengers! How often I have wanted to gather your children together as a hen protects her chicks beneath her wings, but you wouldn't let me. ³⁸And now look, your house is left to you, empty and desolate. ³⁹For I tell you this, you will never see me again until you say, 'Bless the one who comes in the name of the Lord!'*"

CHAPTER 24

Jesus Foretells the Future

As Jesus was leaving the Temple grounds, his disciples pointed out to him the various Temple buildings. ²But he told them, "Do you see all these buildings? I assure you, they will be so completely demolished that not one stone will be left on top of another!"

³Later, Jesus sat on the slopes of the Mount of Olives. His disciples came to him privately and asked, "When will all this take place? And will there be any sign ahead of time to signal your return and the end of the world*?"

⁴Jesus told them, "Don't let anyone mislead you. ⁵For many will come in my name, saying, 'I am the Messiah.' They will lead many astray. ⁶And wars will break out near and far, but don't panic. Yes, these things must come, but the end won't follow immediately. ⁷The nations and kingdoms will proclaim war against each other, and there will be famines

and earthquakes in many parts of the world. [8] But all this will be only the beginning of the horrors to come.

[9] "Then you will be arrested, persecuted, and killed. You will be hated all over the world because of your allegiance to me. [10] And many will turn away from me and betray and hate each other. [11] And many false prophets will appear and will lead many people astray. [12] Sin will be rampant everywhere, and the love of many will grow cold. [13] But those who endure to the end will be saved. [14] And the Good News about the Kingdom will be preached throughout the whole world, so that all nations will hear it; and then, finally, the end will come.

[15] "The time will come when you will see what Daniel the prophet spoke about: the sacrilegious object that causes desecration* standing in the Holy Place"—reader, pay attention! [16] "Then those in Judea must flee to the hills. [17] A person outside the house* must not go inside to pack. [18] A person in the field must not return even to get a coat. [19] How terrible it will be for pregnant women and for mothers nursing their babies in those days. [20] And pray that your flight will not be in winter or on the Sabbath. [21] For that will be a time of greater horror than anything the world has ever seen or will ever see again. [22] In fact, unless that time of calamity is shortened, the entire human race will be destroyed. But it will be shortened for the sake of God's chosen ones.

[23] "Then if anyone tells you, 'Look, here is the Messiah,' or 'There he is,' don't pay any attention. [24] For false messiahs and false prophets will rise up and perform great miraculous signs and wonders so as to deceive, if possible, even God's chosen ones. [25] See, I have warned you.

²⁶"So if someone tells you, 'Look, the Messiah is out in the desert,' don't bother to go and look. Or, 'Look, he is hiding here,' don't believe it! ²⁷For as the lightning lights up the entire sky, so it will be when the Son of Man comes. ²⁸Just as the gathering of vultures shows there is a carcass nearby, so these signs indicate that the end is near.*

²⁹"Immediately after those horrible days end,
the sun will be darkened,
    the moon will not give light,
the stars will fall from the sky,
    and the powers of heaven will be shaken.*

³⁰And then at last, the sign of the coming of the Son of Man will appear in the heavens, and there will be deep mourning among all the nations of the earth. And they will see the Son of Man arrive on the clouds of heaven with power and great glory.* ³¹And he will send forth his angels with the sound of a mighty trumpet blast, and they will gather together his chosen ones from the farthest ends of the earth and heaven.

³²"Now learn a lesson from the fig tree. When its buds become tender and its leaves begin to sprout, you know without being told that summer is near. ³³Just so, when you see the events I've described beginning to happen, you can know his return is very near, right at the door. ³⁴I assure you, this generation* will not pass from the scene before all these things take place. ³⁵Heaven and earth will disappear, but my words will remain for ever.

³⁶"However, no one knows the day or the hour when these things will happen, not even the angels in heaven or the Son himself.* Only the Father knows.

³⁷"When the Son of Man returns, it will be like it was in Noah's day. ³⁸In those days before the Flood, the people

were enjoying banquets and parties and weddings right up to the time Noah entered his boat. ³⁹People didn't realize what was going to happen until the Flood came and swept them all away. That is the way it will be when the Son of Man comes.

⁴⁰"Two men will be working together in the field; one will be taken, the other left. ⁴¹Two women will be grinding flour at the mill; one will be taken, the other left. ⁴²So be prepared, because you don't know what day your Lord is coming.

⁴³"Know this: A home-owner who knew exactly when a burglar was coming would stay alert and not permit the house to be broken into. ⁴⁴You also must be ready all the time. For the Son of Man will come when least expected.

⁴⁵"Who is a faithful, sensible servant, to whom the master can give the responsibility of managing his household and feeding his family? ⁴⁶If the master returns and finds that the servant has done a good job, there will be a reward. ⁴⁷I assure you, the master will put that servant in charge of all he owns. ⁴⁸But if the servant is evil and thinks, 'My master won't be back for a while,' ⁴⁹and begins oppressing the other servants, partying, and getting drunk—⁵⁰well, the master will return unannounced and unexpected. ⁵¹He will tear the servant apart and banish him with the hypocrites. In that place there will be weeping and gnashing of teeth.

CHAPTER 25

Story of the Ten Bridesmaids

"The Kingdom of Heaven can be illustrated by the story of ten bridesmaids* who took their lamps and went to meet the bridegroom. ²Five of them were foolish, and five were wise. ³The five who were foolish took no oil for their lamps,

⁴but the other five were wise enough to take along extra oil. ⁵When the bridegroom was delayed, they all laid down and slept. ⁶At midnight they were roused by the shout, 'Look, the bridegroom is coming! Come out and welcome him!'

⁷"All the bridesmaids got up and prepared their lamps. ⁸Then the five foolish ones asked the others, 'Please give us some of your oil because our lamps are going out.' ⁹But the others replied, 'We don't have enough for all of us. Go to a shop and buy some for yourselves.'

¹⁰"But while they were gone to buy oil, the bridegroom came, and those who were ready went in with him to the marriage feast, and the door was locked. ¹¹Later, when the other five bridesmaids returned, they stood outside, calling, 'Sir, open the door for us!' ¹²But he called back, 'I don't know you!'

¹³"So stay awake and be prepared, because you do not know the day or hour of my return.

Story of the Three Servants

¹⁴"Again, the Kingdom of Heaven can be illustrated by the story of a man going on a trip. He called together his servants and gave them money to invest for him while he was gone. ¹⁵He gave five bags of gold* to one, two bags of gold to another, and one bag of gold to the last—dividing it in proportion to their abilities—and then left on his trip. ¹⁶The servant who received the five bags of gold began immediately to invest the money and soon doubled it. ¹⁷The servant with two bags of gold also went right to work and doubled the money. ¹⁸But the servant who received the one bag of gold dug a hole in the ground and hid the master's money for safe keeping.

¹⁹ "After a long time their master returned from his trip and called them to give an account of how they had used his money. ²⁰ The servant to whom he had entrusted the five bags of gold said, 'Sir, you gave me five bags of gold to invest, and I have doubled the amount.' ²¹ The master was full of praise. 'Well done, my good and faithful servant. You have been faithful in handling this small amount, so now I will give you many more responsibilities. Let's celebrate together!'

²² "Next came the servant who had received the two bags of gold, with the report, 'Sir, you gave me two bags of gold to invest, and I have doubled the amount.' ²³ The master said, 'Well done, my good and faithful servant. You have been faithful in handling this small amount, so now I will give you many more responsibilities. Let's celebrate together!'

²⁴ "Then the servant with the one bag of gold came and said, 'Sir, I know you are a hard man, harvesting crops you didn't plant and gathering crops you didn't cultivate. ²⁵ I was afraid I would lose your money, so I hid it in the earth and here it is.'

²⁶ "But the master replied, 'You wicked and lazy servant! You think I'm a hard man, do you, harvesting crops I didn't plant and gathering crops I didn't cultivate? ²⁷ Well, you should at least have put my money into the bank so I could have some interest. ²⁸ Take the money from this servant and give it to the one with the ten bags of gold. ²⁹ To those who use well what they are given, even more will be given, and they will have an abundance. But from those who are unfaithful,* even what little they have will be taken away. ³⁰ Now throw this useless servant into outer darkness, where there will be weeping and gnashing of teeth.'

The Final Judgement

[31] "But when the Son of Man comes in his glory, and all the angels with him, then he will sit upon his glorious throne. [32] All the nations will be gathered in his presence, and he will separate them as a shepherd separates the sheep from the goats. [33] He will place the sheep at his right hand and the goats at his left. [34] Then the King will say to those on the right, 'Come, you who are blessed by my Father, inherit the Kingdom prepared for you from the foundation of the world. [35] For I was hungry, and you fed me. I was thirsty, and you gave me a drink. I was a stranger, and you invited me into your home. [36] I was naked, and you gave me clothing. I was sick, and you cared for me. I was in prison, and you visited me.'

[37] "Then these righteous ones will reply, 'Lord, when did we ever see you hungry and feed you? Or thirsty and give you something to drink? [38] Or a stranger and show you hospitality? Or naked and give you clothing? [39] When did we ever see you sick or in prison, and visit you?' [40] And the King will tell them, 'I assure you, when you did it to one of the least of these my brothers and sisters,* you were doing it to me!'

[41] "Then the King will turn to those on the left and say, 'Away with you, you cursed ones, into the eternal fire prepared for the Devil and his demons! [42] For I was hungry, and you didn't feed me. I was thirsty, and you didn't give me anything to drink. [43] I was a stranger, and you didn't invite me into your home. I was naked, and you gave me no clothing. I was sick and in prison, and you didn't visit me.'

[44] "Then they will reply, 'Lord, when did we ever see you hungry or thirsty or a stranger or naked or sick or in prison, and not help you?' [45] And he will answer, 'I assure

you, when you refused to help the least of these my brothers and sisters, you were refusing to help me.' ⁴⁶And they will go away into eternal punishment, but the righteous will go into eternal life."

CHAPTER 26

The Plot to Kill Jesus

When Jesus had finished saying these things, he said to his disciples, ²"As you know, the Passover celebration begins in two days, and I, the Son of Man, will be betrayed and crucified."

³At that same time the leading priests and other leaders were meeting at the residence of Caiaphas, the high priest, ⁴to discuss how to capture Jesus secretly and put him to death. ⁵"But not during the Passover," they agreed, "or there will be a riot."

Jesus Anointed at Bethany

⁶Meanwhile, Jesus was in Bethany at the home of Simon, a man who had leprosy. ⁷During supper, a woman came in with a beautiful jar* of expensive perfume and poured it over his head. ⁸The disciples were indignant when they saw this. "What a waste of money," they said. ⁹"She could have sold it for a fortune and given the money to the poor."

¹⁰But Jesus replied, "Why berate her for doing such a good thing to me? ¹¹You will always have the poor among you, but I will not be here with you much longer. ¹²She has poured this perfume on me to prepare my body for burial. ¹³I assure you, wherever the Good News is preached throughout the world, this woman's deed will be talked about in her memory."

Judas Agrees to Betray Jesus

¹⁴Then Judas Iscariot, one of the twelve disciples, went to the leading priests ¹⁵and asked, "How much will you pay me to betray Jesus to you?" And they gave him thirty pieces of silver. ¹⁶From that time on, Judas began looking for the right time and place to betray Jesus.

The Last Supper

¹⁷On the first day of the Festival of Unleavened Bread, the disciples came to Jesus and asked, "Where do you want us to prepare the Passover supper?"

¹⁸"As you go into the city," he told them, "you will see a certain man. Tell him, 'The Teacher says: My time has come, and I will eat the Passover meal with my disciples at your house.'" ¹⁹So the disciples did as Jesus told them and prepared the Passover supper there.

²⁰When it was evening, Jesus sat down at the table with the twelve disciples. ²¹While they were eating, he said, "The truth is, one of you will betray me."

²²Greatly distressed, one by one they began to ask him, "I'm not the one, am I, Lord?"

²³He replied, "One of you who is eating with me now* will betray me. ²⁴For I, the Son of Man, must die, as the Scriptures declared long ago. But how terrible it will be for my betrayer. Far better for him if he had never been born!"

²⁵Judas, the one who would betray him, also asked, "Teacher, I'm not the one, am I?"

And Jesus told him, "You have said it yourself."

²⁶As they were eating, Jesus took a loaf of bread and asked God's blessing on it. Then he broke it in pieces and gave it to the disciples, saying, "Take it and eat it, for this is my body." ²⁷And he took a cup of wine and gave thanks to

God for it. He gave it to them and said, "Each of you drink from it, [28] for this is my blood, which seals the covenant* between God and his people. It is poured out to forgive the sins of many. [29] Mark my words—I will not drink wine again until the day I drink it new with you in my Father's Kingdom." [30] Then they sang a hymn and went out to the Mount of Olives.

Jesus Predicts Peter's Denial

[31] "Tonight all of you will desert me," Jesus told them. "For the Scriptures say,

'God*[b] will strike the Shepherd,
    and the sheep of the flock will be scattered.'*[b]

[32] But after I have been raised from the dead, I will go ahead of you to Galilee and meet you there."

[33] Peter declared, "Even if everyone else deserts you, I never will."

[34] "Peter," Jesus replied, "the truth is, this very night, before the cock crows, you will deny me three times."

[35] "No!" Peter insisted. "Not even if I have to die with you! I will never deny you!" And all the other disciples vowed the same.

Jesus Prays in Gethsemane

[36] Then Jesus brought them to an olive grove called Gethsemane, and he said, "Sit here while I go on ahead to pray." [37] He took Peter and Zebedee's two sons, James and John, and he began to be filled with anguish and deep distress. [38] He told them, "My soul is crushed with grief to the point of death. Stay here and watch with me."

[39] He went on a little farther and fell face down on the ground, praying, "My Father! If it is possible, let this cup of

suffering be taken away from me. Yet I want your will, not mine." ⁴⁰Then he returned to the disciples and found them asleep. He said to Peter, "Couldn't you stay awake and watch with me even one hour? ⁴¹Keep alert and pray. Otherwise temptation will overpower you. For though the spirit is willing enough, the body is weak!"

⁴²Again he left them and prayed, "My Father! If this cup cannot be taken away until I drink it, your will be done." ⁴³He returned to them again and found them sleeping, for they just couldn't keep their eyes open.

⁴⁴So he went back to pray a third time, saying the same things again. ⁴⁵Then he came to the disciples and said, "Still sleeping? Still resting?* Look, the time has come. I, the Son of Man, am betrayed into the hands of sinners. ⁴⁶Up, let's be going. See, my betrayer is here!"

Jesus Is Arrested

⁴⁷And even as he said this, Judas, one of the twelve disciples, arrived with a mob that was armed with swords and clubs. They had been sent out by the leading priests and other leaders of the people. ⁴⁸Judas had given them a pre-arranged signal: "You will know which one to arrest when I go over and give him the kiss of greeting." ⁴⁹So Judas came straight to Jesus. "Greetings, Teacher!" he exclaimed and gave him the kiss.

⁵⁰Jesus said, "My friend, go ahead and do what you have come for." Then the others grabbed Jesus and arrested him. ⁵¹One of the men with Jesus pulled out a sword and slashed off an ear of the high priest's servant.

⁵²"Put away your sword," Jesus told him. "Those who use the sword will be killed by the sword. ⁵³Don't you realize that I could ask my Father for thousands* of angels to

protect us, and he would send them instantly? ⁵⁴But if I did, how would the Scriptures be fulfilled that describe what must happen now?"

⁵⁵Then Jesus said to the crowd, "Am I some dangerous criminal, that you have come armed with swords and clubs to arrest me? Why didn't you arrest me in the Temple? I was there teaching every day. ⁵⁶But this is all happening to fulfil the words of the prophets as recorded in the Scriptures." At that point, all the disciples deserted him and fled.

Jesus before the Council

⁵⁷Then the people who had arrested Jesus led him to the home of Caiaphas, the high priest, where the teachers of religious law and other leaders had gathered. ⁵⁸Meanwhile, Peter was following far behind and eventually came to the courtyard of the high priest's house. He went in, sat with the guards, and waited to see what was going to happen to Jesus.

⁵⁹Inside, the leading priests and the entire high council* were trying to find witnesses who would lie about Jesus, so they could put him to death. ⁶⁰But even though they found many who agreed to give false witness, there was no testimony they could use. Finally, two men were found ⁶¹who declared, "This man said, 'I am able to destroy the Temple of God and rebuild it in three days.'"

⁶²Then the high priest stood up and said to Jesus, "Well, aren't you going to answer these charges? What do you have to say for yourself?" ⁶³But Jesus remained silent. Then the high priest said to him, "I demand in the name of the living God that you tell us whether you are the Messiah, the Son of God."

⁶⁴Jesus replied, "Yes, it is as you say. And in the future you will see me, the Son of Man, sitting at God's right hand in the place of power and coming back on the clouds of heaven."*

⁶⁵Then the high priest tore his clothing to show his horror, shouting, "Blasphemy! Why do we need other witnesses? You have all heard his blasphemy. ⁶⁶What is your verdict?"

"Guilty!" they shouted. "He must die!"

⁶⁷Then they spat in Jesus' face and hit him with their fists. And some slapped him, ⁶⁸saying, "Prophesy to us, you Messiah! Who hit you that time?"

Peter Denies Jesus

⁶⁹Meanwhile, as Peter was sitting outside in the courtyard, a servant girl came over and said to him, "You were one of those with Jesus the Galilean."

⁷⁰But Peter denied it in front of everyone. "I don't know what you are talking about," he said.

⁷¹Later, out by the gate, another servant girl noticed him and said to those standing around, "This man was with Jesus of Nazareth."

⁷²Again Peter denied it, this time with an oath. "I don't even know the man," he said.

⁷³A little later some other bystanders came over to him and said, "You must be one of them; we can tell by your Galilean accent."

⁷⁴Peter said, "I swear by God, I don't know the man." And immediately the cock crowed. ⁷⁵Suddenly, Jesus' words flashed through Peter's mind: "Before the cock crows, you will deny me three times." And he went away, crying bitterly.

CHAPTER 27

Judas Hangs Himself

Very early in the morning, the leading priests and other leaders met again to discuss how to persuade the Roman government to sentence Jesus to death. ²Then they bound him and took him to Pilate, the Roman governor.

³When Judas, who had betrayed him, realized that Jesus had been condemned to die, he was filled with remorse. So he took the thirty pieces of silver back to the leading priests and other leaders. ⁴"I have sinned," he declared, "for I have betrayed an innocent man."

"What do we care?" they retorted. "That's your problem."
⁵Then Judas threw the money onto the floor of the Temple and went out and hanged himself. ⁶The leading priests picked up the money. "We can't put it in the Temple treasury," they said, "since it's against the law to accept money paid for murder." ⁷After some discussion they finally decided to buy the potter's field, and they made it into a cemetery for foreigners. ⁸That is why the field is still called the Field of Blood. ⁹This fulfilled the prophecy of Jeremiah that says,

"They took* the thirty pieces of silver—
    the price at which he was valued by the people of
      Israel—
¹⁰ and purchased the potter's field,
    as the Lord directed.*"

Jesus' Trial before Pilate

¹¹Now Jesus was standing before Pilate, the Roman governor. "Are you the King of the Jews?" the governor asked him.

Jesus replied, "Yes, it is as you say."

¹²But when the leading priests and other leaders made their accusations against him, Jesus remained silent. ¹³"Don't you hear their many charges against you?" Pilate demanded. ¹⁴But Jesus said nothing, much to the governor's great surprise.

¹⁵Now it was the governor's custom to release one prisoner to the crowd each year during the Passover celebration—anyone they wanted. ¹⁶This year there was a notorious criminal in prison, a man named Barabbas.* ¹⁷As the crowds gathered before Pilate's house that morning, he asked them, "Which one do you want me to release to you—Barabbas, or Jesus who is called the Messiah?" ¹⁸(He knew very well that the Jewish leaders had arrested Jesus out of envy.)

¹⁹Just then, as Pilate was sitting on the judgement seat, his wife sent him this message: "Leave that innocent man alone, because I had a terrible nightmare about him last night."

²⁰Meanwhile, the leading priests and other leaders persuaded the crowds to ask for Barabbas to be released and for Jesus to be put to death. ²¹So when the governor asked again, "Which of these two do you want me to release to you?" the crowd shouted back their reply: "Barabbas!"

²²"But if I release Barabbas," Pilate asked them, "what should I do with Jesus who is called the Messiah?"

And they all shouted, "Crucify him!"

²³"Why?" Pilate demanded. "What crime has he committed?"

But the crowd only roared the louder, "Crucify him!"

²⁴ Pilate saw that he wasn't getting anywhere and that a riot was developing. So he sent for a bowl of water and washed his hands before the crowd, saying, "I am innocent of the blood of this man. The responsibility is yours!"

²⁵ And all the people yelled back, "We will take responsibility for his death—we and our children!"*

²⁶ So Pilate released Barabbas to them. He ordered Jesus flogged with a lead-tipped whip, then turned him over to the Roman soldiers to crucify him.

The Soldiers Mock Jesus

²⁷ Some of the governor's soldiers took Jesus into their headquarters and called out the entire battalion. ²⁸ They stripped him and put a scarlet robe on him. ²⁹ They made a crown of long, sharp thorns and put it on his head, and they placed a stick in his right hand as a sceptre. Then they knelt before him in mockery, yelling, "Hail! King of the Jews!" ³⁰ And they spat on him and grabbed the stick and beat him on the head with it. ³¹ When they were finally tired of mocking him, they took off the robe and put his own clothes on him again. Then they led him away to be crucified.

The Crucifixion

³² Along the way, they came across a man named Simon, who was from Cyrene,* and they forced him to carry Jesus' cross. ³³ Then they went out to a place called Golgotha (which means Skull Hill). ³⁴ The soldiers gave him wine mixed with bitter gall, but when he had tasted it, he refused to drink it.

³⁵ After they had nailed him to the cross, the soldiers gambled for his clothes by throwing dice.* ³⁶ Then they sat around and kept guard as he hung there. ³⁷ A signboard

was fastened to the cross above Jesus' head, announcing the charge against him. It read: "This is Jesus, the King of the Jews."

[38]Two criminals were crucified with him, their crosses on either side of his. [39]And the people passing by shouted abuse, shaking their heads in mockery. [40]"So! You can destroy the Temple and build it again in three days, can you? Well then, if you are the Son of God, save yourself and come down from the cross!"

[41]The leading priests, the teachers of religious law, and the other leaders also mocked Jesus. [42]"He saved others," they scoffed, "but he can't save himself! So he is the king of Israel, is he? Let him come down from the cross, and we will believe in him! [43]He trusted God—let God show his approval by delivering him! For he said, 'I am the Son of God.'" [44]And the criminals who were crucified with him also shouted the same insults at him.

The Death of Jesus

[45]At noon, darkness fell across the whole land until three o'clock. [46]At about three o'clock, Jesus called out with a loud voice, "*Eli, Eli, lema sabachthani?*" which means, "My God, my God, why have you forsaken me?"*

[47]Some of the bystanders misunderstood and thought he was calling for the prophet Elijah. [48]One of them ran and filled a sponge with sour wine, holding it up to him on a stick so he could drink. [49]But the rest said, "Leave him alone. Let's see whether Elijah will come and save him."*

[50]Then Jesus shouted out again, and he gave up his spirit. [51]At that moment the curtain in the Temple was torn in two, from top to bottom. The earth shook, rocks split apart, [52]and tombs opened. The bodies of many

godly men and women who had died were raised from the dead [53] after Jesus' resurrection. They left the cemetery, went into the holy city of Jerusalem, and appeared to many people.*

[54] The Roman officer and the other soldiers at the crucifixion were terrified by the earthquake and all that had happened. They said, "Truly, this was the Son of God!"

[55] And many women who had come from Galilee with Jesus to care for him were watching from a distance. [56] Among them were Mary Magdalene, Mary (the mother of James and Joseph), and Zebedee's wife, the mother of James and John.

The Burial of Jesus

[57] As evening approached, Joseph, a rich man from Arimathea who was one of Jesus' followers, [58] went to Pilate and asked for Jesus' body. And Pilate issued an order to release it to him. [59] Joseph took the body and wrapped it in a long linen cloth. [60] He placed it in his own new tomb, which had been carved out of the rock. Then he rolled a great stone across the entrance as he left. [61] Both Mary Magdalene and the other Mary were sitting nearby watching.

The Guard at the Tomb

[62] The next day—on the first day of the Passover ceremonies*—the leading priests and Pharisees went to see Pilate. [63] They told him, "Sir, we remember what that deceiver once said while he was still alive: 'After three days I will be raised from the dead.' [64] So we request that you seal the tomb until the third day. This will prevent his disciples from coming and stealing his body and then

telling everyone he came back to life! If that happens, we'll be worse off than we were at first."

⁶⁵ Pilate replied, "Take guards and secure it the best you can." ⁶⁶ So they sealed the tomb and posted guards to protect it.

CHAPTER 28

The Resurrection

Early on Sunday morning,* as the new day was dawning, Mary Magdalene and the other Mary went out to see the tomb. ² Suddenly there was a great earthquake, because an angel of the Lord came down from heaven and rolled aside the stone and sat on it. ³ His face shone like lightning, and his clothing was as white as snow. ⁴ The guards shook with fear when they saw him, and they fell into a dead faint.

⁵ Then the angel spoke to the women. "Don't be afraid!" he said. "I know you are looking for Jesus, who was crucified. ⁶ He isn't here! He has been raised from the dead, just as he said would happen. Come, see where his body was lying. ⁷ And now, go quickly and tell his disciples he has been raised from the dead, and he is going ahead of you to Galilee. You will see him there. Remember, I have told you."

⁸ The women ran quickly from the tomb. They were very frightened but also filled with great joy, and they rushed to find the disciples to give them the angel's message. ⁹ And as they went, Jesus met them. "Greetings!" he said. And they ran to him, held his feet, and worshipped him. ¹⁰ Then Jesus said to them, "Don't be afraid! Go tell my brothers to leave for Galilee, and they will see me there."

The Report of the Guard

[11] As the women were on their way into the city, some of the men who had been guarding the tomb went to the leading priests and told them what had happened. [12] A meeting of all the religious leaders was called, and they decided to bribe the soldiers. [13] They told the soldiers, "You must say, 'Jesus' disciples came during the night while we were sleeping, and they stole his body.' [14] If the governor hears about it, we'll stand up for you and everything will be all right." [15] So the guards accepted the bribe and said what they were told to say. Their story spread widely among the Jews, and they still tell it today.

The Great Commission

[16] Then the eleven disciples left for Galilee, going to the mountain where Jesus had told them to go. [17] When they saw him, they worshipped him—but some of them still doubted! [18] Jesus came and told his disciples, "I have been given complete authority in heaven and on earth. [19] Therefore, go and make disciples of all the nations, baptizing them in the name of the Father and the Son and the Holy Spirit. [20] Teach these new disciples to obey all the commands I have given you. And be sure of this: I am with you always, even to the end of the age."

Footnotes

Chapter 1

1:3 Greek *Aram;* also in 1:4. See 1 Chr 2:9–10.
1:7 *Asaph* is the same person as Asa; also in 1:8. See 1 Chr 3:10.
1:8a Greek *Joram.* See 1 Kgs 22:50 and note at 1 Chr 3:11.
1:8b Or *ancestor;* also in 1:11.
1:10 *Amos* is the same person as Amon. See 1 Chr 3:14.
1:11 Greek *Jeconiah;* also in 1:12. See 2 Kgs 24:6 and note at 1 Chr 3:16.
1:21 *Jesus* means "The LORD saves."
1:23 Isa 7:14; 8:8, 10.

Chapter 2

2:1 Or *royal astrologers;* Greek reads *magi;* also in 2:7, 16.
2:2 Or *in the east.*
2:6 Mic 5:2; 2 Sam 5:2.
2:15 Hos 11:1
2:16 Or *according to the time he calculated from the wise men.*
2:18 Jer 31:15

Chapter 3

3:2 Or *has come,* or *is coming soon.*
3:3 Isa 40:3
3:11a Or *in.*
3:11b Greek *to carry his sandals.*
3:11c Or *in the Holy Spirit and in fire.*
3:15 Or *we must fulfil all righteousness.*

Chapter 4

4:3 Greek *the tempter.*
4:4 Deut 8:3
4:6 Ps 91:11–12
4:7 Deut 6:16
4:10 Deut 6:13
4:15–16 Isa 9:1–2
4:17 Or *has come,* or *is coming soon.*
4:25 Greek *Decapolis.*

Chapter 5

5:3 Greek *the poor in spirit.*
5:21 Exod 20:13; Deut 5:17.
5:22a Some manuscripts add *without cause.*
5:22b Greek uses an Aramaic term of contempt: *If you say to your brother, 'Raca.'*
5:22c Greek *if you say, 'You fool.'*
5:27 Exod 20:14; Deut 5:18.
5:29 Greek *your right eye.*
5:30 Greek *your right hand.*
5:31 Deut 24:1
5:33 Num 30:2
5:37 Or *Anything beyond this is from the evil one.*
5:38 Greek *'An eye for an eye and a tooth for a tooth.'* Exod 21:24; Lev 24:20; Deut 19:21.
5:41 Greek *milion* [1.5 kilometres or 4,854 feet].
5:43 Lev 19:18
5:44 Some manuscripts add *Bless those who curse you, do good to those who hate you.*
5:47 Greek *your brothers.*

Chapter 6

6:11 Or *for tomorrow.*
6:13 Or *from evil.* Some manuscripts add *For yours is the kingdom and the power and the glory for ever. Amen.*

Chapter 7

7:2 Or *For God will treat you as you treat others;* Greek reads *For with the judgement you judge, you will be judged.*
7:3 Greek *your brother's eye;* also in 7:5.
7:6 Greek *Don't give the sacred to dogs.*
7:13 Greek *The way that leads to destruction.*
7:23 Or *unlawful.*

Chapter 8

8:17 Isa 53:4
8:22 Greek *Let the dead bury their own dead.*
8:28 Some manuscripts read *Gerasenes;* other manuscripts read *Gergesenes.* See Mark 5:1; Luke 8:26.

Chapter 9

9:11 Greek *with tax collectors and sinners.*
9:13 Hos 6:6

Chapter 10

10:4 Greek *the Cananean.*
10:7 Or *has come,* or *is coming soon.*
10:10 Or *the worker is worthy of support.*
10:25 Greek *Beelzeboul.*
10:41 Greek *welcome a prophet in the name of a prophet.*

Chapter 11

11:6 Or *who don't fall away because of me.*
11:10 Mal 3:1
11:12 Or *until now, eager multitudes have been pressing into the Kingdom of Heaven.*
11:14 See Mal 4:5
11:23 Greek *to Hades.*

Chapter 12

12:7 Hos 6:6
12:18–21 Isa 42:1–4
12:24 Greek *Beelzeboul.*
12:27 Greek *by Beelzeboul.*
12:29 Or *One cannot rob Satan's kingdom without first tying him up. Only then can his demons be cast out.*
12:42 Greek *The queen of the south.*

Chapter 13

13:14–15 Isa 6:9–10
13:33 Greek *3 measures.*
13:35 Ps 78:2.

Chapter 14

14:1 Greek *Herod the tetrarch.* He was a son of King Herod and was ruler over one of the four districts in Palestine.
14:25 Greek *In the fourth watch of the night.*

Chapter 15

15:4 Exod 20:12; 21:17; Lev 20:9; Deut 5:16.
15:8-9 Isa 29:13
15:11 Or *what comes out of the mouth defiles a person.*
15:22 Greek *Canaanite.*

Chapter 16

16:2-3 Several manuscripts do not include any of the words in 16:2-3 after *He replied.*
16:17 Greek *Simon son of Jonah;* see John 1:42; 21:15-17.
16:18a *Peter* means "stone" or "rock."
16:18b Greek *and the gates of Hades.*
16:26 Or *your life;* also in 16:26b.

Chapter 17

17:4 Or *shelters;* Greek reads *tabernacles.*
17:10 Greek *that Elijah must come first.*
17:20 Some manuscripts add verse 21, *But this kind of demon won't leave unless you have prayed and fasted.*
17:25 Greek *Simon.*

Chapter 18

18:8 Greek *enter life;* also in 18:9.
18:10 Some manuscripts add verse 11, *And I, the Son of Man, have come to save the lost.*
18:15 Greek *your brother.*
18:20 Greek *gather together in my name.*
18:21 Greek *my brother.*
18:22 Or *77 times.*
18:24 Greek *10,000 talents.*
18:28 Greek *100 denarii.* A denarius was the equivalent of a full day's wage.
18:35 Greek *your brother.*

Chapter 19

19:4 Gen 1:27; 5:2.
19:5 Gen 2:24
19:7 Deut 24:1
19:9 Some manuscripts add *And the man who marries a divorced woman commits adultery.*
19:16 Some manuscripts read *Good Teacher.*
19:18–19 Exod 20:12–16; Lev 19:18; Deut 5:16–20.
19:28 Greek *in the regeneration.*
19:30 Greek *But many who are first will be last; and the last, first.*

Chapter 20

20:2 Greek *a denarius,* the payment for a full day's labour; also in 20:9, 10, 13.

Chapter 21

21:5a Greek *Tell the daughter of Zion.* Isa 62:11.
21:5b Zech 9:9
21:7 Greek *over them, and he sat on them.*
21:9a Greek *Hosanna,* an exclamation of praise that literally means "save now"; also in 21:9b, 15.
21:9b Pss 118:25–26; 148:1.
21:13 Isa 56:7; Jer 7:11.
21:16 Ps 8:2
21:23 Or *By whose authority do you do these things?*
21:42 Ps 118:22–23
21:44 This verse is omitted in some early manuscripts.

Chapter 22

22:19 Greek *a denarius.*
22:24 Deut 25:5–6
22:31 Greek *in the Scriptures? God said.*
22:32 Exod 3:6
22:37 Deut 6:5
22:39 Lev 19:18
22:44 Ps 110:1

Chapter 23

23:5 Greek *They enlarge their phylacteries.*
23:7 *Rabbi*, from Aramaic, means "master" or "teacher."
23:8 Greek *brothers.*
23:13 Some manuscripts add verse 14, *How terrible it will be for you teachers of religious law and you Pharisees. Hypocrites! You shamelessly cheat widows out of their property, and then, to cover up the kind of people you really are, you make long prayers in public. Because of this, your punishment will be the greater.*
23:23 Greek *to tithe the mint, the dill, and the cumin.*
23:39 Ps 118:26

Chapter 24

24:3 Or *the age.*
24:15 Greek *the abomination of desolation.* See Dan 9:27; 11:31; 12:11.
24:17 Greek *on the roof.*
24:28 Greek *Wherever the carcass is, the vultures gather.*
24:29 See Isa 13:10; 34:4; Joel 2:10.
24:30 See Dan 7:13.
24:34 Or *this age,* or *this nation.*
24:36 Some manuscripts omit the phrase *or the Son himself.*

Chapter 25

25:1 Or *virgins;* also in 25:7, 11.
25:15 Greek *talents;* also throughout the story. A talent is equal to 34 kilograms or 75 pounds.
25:29 Or *who have nothing.*
25:40 Greek *my brothers.*

Chapter 26

26:7 Greek *an alabaster jar.*
26:23 Or *The one who has dipped his hand in the bowl with me.*
26:28 Some manuscripts read *the new covenant.*
26:31a Greek *I.*
26:31b Zech 13:7
26:45 Or *Sleep on, take your rest.*
26:53 Greek *12 legions.*
26:59 Greek *the Sanhedrin.*
26:64 See Ps 110:1; Dan 7:13.

Chapter 27

27:9 Or *I took.*
27:9-10 Greek *as the Lord directed me.* Zech 11:12–13; Jer 32:6–9.
27:16 Some manuscripts read *Jesus Barabbas;* also in 27:17.
27:25 Greek *"His blood be on us and on our children."*
27:32 *Cyrene* was a city in northern Africa.
27:35 Greek *by casting lots.* A few late manuscripts add *This fulfilled the word of the prophet: "They divided my clothes among themselves and cast lots for my robe."* See Ps 22:18.
27:46 Ps 22:1
27:49 Some manuscripts add *And another took a spear and pierced his side, and out came water and blood.*
27:51-53 Or *The earth shook, rocks split apart, tombs opened, and the bodies of many godly men and women who had died were raised from the dead. After Jesus' resurrection, they left the cemetery, went into the holy city of Jerusalem, and appeared to many people.*
27:62 Or *On the next day, which is after the Preparation.*

Chapter 28

28:1 Greek *After the Sabbath, on the first day of the week.*